HOW DO I KNOW I'M SAVED?

A Study of God's Grace

D1522901

HOW DO I KNOW I'M SAVED?

A Study of God's Grace

While this book has been written for group studies, it is also intended for your personal enjoyment.

NORMAN L. BALES

Christian Communications
P.O. Box 150
Nashville, Tennessee 37202

Published by Gospel Advocate Co.
P. O. Box 150, Nashville, TN 37202

ISBN 0-89225-349-5

Second Printing 1991

This book
is dedicated to
Dr. J. D. Thomas
and
Dr. Frank Pack,
two of my early mentors in the faith.
They first introduced me to grace
as a positive doctrine.

Foreword

The ideal of restoration implies the recovery of apostolic Christianity in its entirety. We in the heritage of the Restoration Movement have stressed the restitution of the church, but have tended to overlook other teachings which are equally important. One of these themes is the grace of God. This lack of attention to such a vital subject is reflected in the few books that have dealt with it.

The need for a better appreciation of grace is seen when we fail to realize that divine grace is more than an isolated act of redemption. It is also a state in which God's children daily live. We sometimes develop a kind of perfectionism which leads us to believe that God will not forgive certain kinds of moral or doctrinal sins. This failure to understand the nature of grace also contributes to the uncertainty of salvation which many Christians feel.

Sometime ago Norman Bales sent me an outline of a course on grace that he had prepared. I was so impressed by the content of his lessons that I urged him to put his material into printed form. This book is the result. Whether your appreciation of the grace of God is great or small, *How Do I Know I'm Saved?* will broaden your understanding of our salvation.

—Monroe E. Hawley

Contents

Introduction

"If I were to die right now, I don't think I'd go to heaven." The woman who said that to me grew up in a Christian home. She'd heard so many gospel sermons that she could easily anticipate the preacher's next point. In her formative years, she listened to issue-oriented preaching with a strong focus on obedience. She took it all very seriously, and she worked hard at being an obedient Christian. If she didn't attend the assembly, all the other members knew it meant she was out of town or that she was ill. Her beliefs and moral standards would have been acceptable to the most conservative advocate of sound doctrine.

She had explored the subject of grace enough to intellectually comprehend the concept that man cannot be his own savior. Nevertheless, she was disturbed about her spiritual condition. She had never developed a secure relationship with God. The "peace that passes understanding" was a goal she longed to realize, but it eluded her. Her insecurity stemmed from uncertainty about the assurance of her personal salvation.

This fine lady is really a composite of many Christians, both male and female, who take their responsibility to the Lord seriously. They are honest enough to recognize flaws in their discipleship, but they really don't understand how God's grace reaches them. They may well have the academic aspects of grace, but they really don't feel saved. They've been victimized by our reluctance to present a positive view of grace from the pulpit and in the class-room.

One would think that those Christians living out the twilight years of their lives would be the most confident believers. In fact, I don't hear many of our more senior brothers and sisters who sound like Paul did in 2 Timothy 4:7-8 as he wrote, "I have fought the good fight, I have finished the race, I have kept the faith. Now there is in store for me the crown of righteousness, which the Lord, the righteous Judge, will award to me on that day—and not only to me, but also to all who have longed for his appearing." When the apostle was ready to face the executioner's sword, he exhibited courage because his eyes were focused on an eternal crown that he confidently expected to receive.

When Christians who have been faithful throughout their lives feel compelled to ask, "Do you think I'm good enough for God to let me into heaven?" then it's time to take another look at the emphasis in our teaching programs. Eddie Messer observes,

> What I find most alarming is that many of these souls are not only discouraged . . . they even doubt their salvation! That is tragic! It frightens me that Christian people who live their whole life for the Lord can enter the sunset years in fear and doubt. Can this be the price we pay for not teaching on God's grace?![1]

Within the Christian community, we need to be challenged to rethink God's reasons for communicating with mankind. His message is not this: "I'm going to show you how I can run over you. I'm going to complicate your life with problems, then I'm going to put obstacles in your path to make your life difficult. But I'll reluctantly allow you into heaven—provided you have sufficient strength of character to clear all the hurdles." Instead, God's essential message to the world is this: "For God so loved the world that he gave his one and only Son, that whoever believes in him shall not perish but have eternal life" (John 3:16). At great cost to Himself, God has devised a program that will enable imperfect people to rise above their flaws, experience forgiveness of their sins, and live in joyous anticipation of sharing an eternal home with Him.

The process by which God's love is translated into action is called *grace*. Unlike the word *love (agape)*, the term *grace (charis)* wasn't coined by the Christian community. The word was commonly used among the Greek-speaking people of the first century and generally served as a synonym for words like *favor, charm,* and *attractiveness*.[2] Quite a few times, the word appears in the New Testament to express thoughts of gratitude and thankfulness. It's from this usage that many Christian families have come to call their prayer of thanksgiving at mealtime a *table grace*. In a sense, everything we enjoy flows from God's grace: "Every good and perfect gift is from above, coming down from the Father of the heavenly lights, who does not change like shifting shadows" (James 1:17).

In this study, however, *grace* will be rather narrowly applied to describe God's active love for people. The magnitude of our study forces us to admit that our keenest perceptions scarcely penetrate the surface of a profound truth reservoir. Nevertheless, we should be challenged to drink as deeply from the fountain of grace as our capabilities will allow. Our goal is to grow in grace as well as in knowledge (2 Peter 1:3).

Notes

[1]Eddie Messer, "Grace and the Aged," *Image*, November 1, 1985, p. 6.

[2]J. I. Packer, *Knowing God* (Downers Grove, Ill.: Intervarsity Press, 1973), p. 116.

C H A P T E R 1

Why We Need
a Savior

Sometimes our Christian vocabulary hinders our ability to communicate effectively with the non-Christian world. A lady who bore heavy burdens was encouraged to investigate Christianity. She chose a church at random and happened to end up at an assembly where the worship structure was fairly loose. Sometimes the preacher carried on a dialogue with his audience. On her first visit, the preacher said, "If you'd like to be saved, hold up your hand." The woman later recalled, "I just sat there. I didn't know what 'saved' meant. I knew I wasn't in any kind of physical danger. Of course, the man was talking about forgiveness, but his message went right over my head."

When the minister asked individuals who wanted to be saved to so indicate, he touched on the most urgent human need. Unfortunately, the word *saved* doesn't connect with the kind of thought patterns that have developed in the non-Christian mind. A person may realize that the word is somehow associated with a sort of in-house vocabulary used almost exclusively in the Christian community, but he doesn't understand it any more than an untrained person can comprehend a medically oriented discussion between physicians. Before we can effectively communicate the message of grace, we have to find a way to overcome the roadblocks to understanding that have been placed in the path of the truth seekers as the result of terminology.

The salvation idea must be grasped because without it, people can never come to appreciate what Jesus can do for them. When Jesus came into our world, the angels told the shepherds, "Today in the town of David a *Savior* has been born to you; he is Christ the Lord" (Luke 2:11, emphasis added). It's important to understand both what a Savior does and why each one of us needs a Savior.

The Reality of Sin

Responsible people reach a time in their lives when their thinking ability develops to the point that they are able to distinguish between right and wrong. We need a Savior because all accountable people fall victim to a malignant killer that destroys the inward personality and alienates the individual from God. The biblical name for this spiritual cancer is *sin*. I'm going to bypass the technical jargon fueling so much theological debate and simply say that sin encompasses all the behavior patterns, actions, and attitudes that don't measure up to what God expects from people.

Both Old and New Testaments refer repeatedly to the universality of sin. When Solomon dedicated the ancient Hebrew temple in Jerusalem, he said, "There is no one who does not sin" (1 Kings 8:46). The psalmist certainly comprehended the pervasiveness of the problem: "If you, O LORD, kept a record of sins, O Lord, who could stand?" (Psalm 130:3). Isaiah removed all human defense mechanisms when he stated,

> All of us have become like one who is unclean,
>   and all our righteous acts are like filthy rags;
> we all shrivel up like a leaf,
>   and like the wind our sins sweep us away (Isaiah 64:6).

The Old Testament portrait of sin presents a bleak view of human desperation.

In the New Testament, the first three chapters of Romans are devoted to documenting the universality of sin. Every attempt at human justification and evasive rationalization is exploded in Romans 3:9 when Paul concludes "that Jews and Gentiles alike are all under sin." Even the Christian who has overcome sin through the work of Jesus Christ must admit the presence of sin in his life: "If we confess our sins, he is faithful and just and will forgive us our sins and purify us from all unrighteousness. If we claim we have not sinned, we make him out to be a liar and his word has no place in our lives" (1 John 1:9-10).

Human experience agrees with the documentation of Scripture. Some time ago, a licensed electrician talked with me about municipal wiring codes. He said, "When you try to move around the country, it's very frustrating because every locality has different codes and you have to pass a test on each individual community code to get a license."

I said, "If it's all that confused, then why doesn't Congress simply outlaw all these codes?"

He was shocked at my ignorance. He said, "Norman, do you realize that you'd be inviting electrical disaster if you did away with codes? Electricians would take shortcuts to save a dollar here and there. The do-it-yourself amateurs would come up with all kinds of Mickey Mouse wiring procedures. Fires caused by electricity would get

out of hand. Helpless children would be burned to death
in apartments and houses because of careless wiring.
You've got to have electrical codes to protect man from
his own stupidity."

Of course, he's right. When people are left to their
own devices, they usually behave irresponsibly. Because
we recognize the evil tendency in people, we find it
necessary to hire a police force and construct jails. We
don't actually have to read the biblical pronouncements
about sin to realize that something has gummed up the
works in human behavior. Our experience in every area
of life confirms the reality of man's perverse behavior.

Reaction to Sin

People react to the problem of sin in several different
ways. Some choose *denial*. In recent years, the person
who indicts his fellow human beings and seeks to convict
them of having wronged God has been treated almost as
if he were unpatriotic, or as a busybody who doesn't
know how to mind his own business. Today's secularized
person often perceives sin as a superstitious relic of the
unenlightened past. Some people think the sin idea
should go the way of the witchcraft trials. They view it
as a painful and unnecessary part of human history. These
days sin is caricatured as a manipulative tool of fundamen-
talist firebrands.

There is no defense for the minister who participates
in immoral excesses during the week and condemns
immorality on Sunday. There is no way to justly rationalize the behavior of a preacher who employs guilt tripping
as a device to satisfy his personal power urges. We must
understand, however, that preachers didn't invent the sin

concept. Although sin may be ridiculed and denied by the clever sophists of our age, modern rhetoric doesn't change the fact that sin destroys relationships, robs us of personal happiness, and contributes to the misery that hangs on to the human race like an incurable illness. We're all affected by the sin problem, and we can't participate in the blessings of God's grace if we continue to deny the existence of personal sin.

Bringing men and women to a consciousness of sin is a necessary part of the salvation process. Some unscrupulous religious figures use this realization as a kind of power lever to control people. The legitimate way of realization is illustrated by the interaction of physician and patient. A physician diagnoses disease to facilitate healing. He may tell a patient that cancer cells have invaded the body. That's always bad news, but the doctor doesn't talk about the cancer in order to gain a position of control over the patient. The patient cannot be persuaded to undergo chemotherapy, radiation treatments, or surgery unless he knows that a dangerous malignancy threatens his life and that these forms of treatment may bring about a possible cure or a remission of the disease. Convicting people of sin serves the same purpose in helping them to understand Jesus' offer to provide spiritual healing. This is why Jesus said the Holy Spirit would "convict the world of guilt in regard to sin and righteousness and judgment" (John 16:8).

Rationalization is another popular response to sin and is evident in statements like, "What I'm doing may be wrong, but it's not nearly as immoral as the sins of my neighbor." Sometimes, rationalization surfaces through an admission followed by the claim that a person ought to be allowed a certain quota of sins. People don't usually say it just that way, however. The explanation comes out something like this: "Well, I know what I'm doing is wrong, but after all, I have only this one vice." Some people understand the doctrine of grace to cover their intentional disobedience. That's what a person is doing who says, "Surely God wants me to be happy, and even if the Bible does condemn what I'm doing, I don't think I'll go to hell for it. Surely God doesn't want me to go through this life being miserable, and He knows I can't be happy unless I indulge myself in this particular vice."

The power of the human mind to rationalize literally knows no limits. Christians must remember that an evil personality inhabits this world who specializes in deception. He "masquerades as an angel of light" (2 Corinthians 11:14). It is essential to openly accept the reality of our sins because we block God's grace from our lives when we try to excuse them. Dietrich Bonhoeffer observed, "Human nature moves toward self-justification. Sin is in every instance something quite concrete. It must be identified by name. Only the demon which is called by name departs."[1]

Procrastination prevents many people from confronting their sins. There are some who feel the full force of personal guilt. They understand their need to repent. They've been bludgeoned from the pulpit and even told the preachers who applied the tongue-lashing, "I needed that." They may further understand that sin can be removed only by the blood of Jesus. Someday, they plan to deal with it, but they refuse to be specific about which future date will be reserved for that purpose. They're waiting for things to settle down, so they can get their priorities sorted out. One person may be thinking, *I'll deal with sin when I'm finished with school.* Another is putting it off until marriage. Someone else is waiting until after the baby comes, and so it goes. For some, it seems like the golden moment of opportunity is some nebulous date in a far distant future. One is reminded of Felix as he put off Paul by saying, "When I find it convenient, I will send for you" (Acts 24:25). Apparently, the convenient time never arrived for Felix.

Still others attempt to handle the sin problem by *pretending to be perfect.* They're good, moral people. They don't commit adultery. They don't cheat and lie. They go to worship. They live responsible lives. They may be aware of a few flaws here and there, but like Mary Poppins, they consider themselves "practically perfect people." They have little awareness of their need for a Savior because they don't see a dark side of their character. They may be blind to their selfishness, their arrogance, or their self-righteousness. They're in the church, but their focus is on themselves, not on Jesus.

Results of Sin

If people insist on resisting the Savior through such unhealthy responses, calamitous results will inevitably follow. Consider some of the debilitating effects the persistent practice of sin has on our lives.

1. *Sin destroys fellowship with God.* John writes, "This is the message we have heard from him and declare to you: God is light; in him there is no darkness at all. If we claim to have fellowship with him yet talk in the darkness, we lie and do not live by the truth" (1 John 1:5-6). There's a vacuum in the human soul that causes us to hunger for fellowship with our Maker. Sin severs the umbilical cord giving life to that relationship.

2. *Sin deprives us of our personal freedom.* Many persons turn away from Christ because it seems to them that His demand for a disciplined life robs them of their freedom. Freedom is such a cherished value that men have often sacrificed their lives in an effort to ensure the freedom of others. The person who wants to live according to his own impulses perceives Christ to be a threat to that precious freedom. He asks, "Why can't I do what *I* please?"

In a sense, we must concede the logic of the person who wants to have things his own way. The Scriptures even acknowledge that the libertine has a legitimate point. In Romans 6:20, Paul says, "When you were slaves to sin, you were free from the control of righteousness." Observe, however, that Paul identifies the person who is addicted to the practice of sin as a slave. Slaves aren't free people. Whether the person who wants to please himself realizes it or not, he is a slave to his own appetites and passions. He is not free to discipline himself in the performance of those acts that are noble and honorable.

I have a friend who works as a commercial pilot for a major airline. He is free to do something I can't do. He can climb into the cockpit, taxi down the runway, and ease that big silver jet into the sky. That's freedom, but it's freedom that was gained through self-denial. He had to undertake the discipline of rigid flight training before being entrusted with a multimillion-dollar aircraft and the lives of the passengers who fly with him. His willingness to undergo the strict regimentation of flight training won him his license to fly. The Christian may face some restrictions in his life, but the restrictions are there to give greater freedom, not to inhibit the enjoyment of worthwhile things.

3. *Sin produces death.* In Romans 6:23, Paul says that "the wages of sin is death." A student who enrolls in a college course can either choose to complete his assignments or neglect them. If he so chooses, he can spend his evenings attending movies, watching television, or racking up balls at the pool hall. He doesn't have to write papers, study for tests, and pay attention in class. He can sneer at the "bookworms" who burn the midnight oil, complete assignments on time, take notes in class, and receive A's for their efforts. He has no ground for complaint when his own grade point average dips below an acceptable level. An undisciplined approach to classroom study requires a price of the student—that of receiving a low grade.

The freedom that comes with a life devoted to sin is similar. The undisciplined student may appear to be getting away with his casual attitude toward study, but the grades are given out at the end of the course, not at the end of the first week. If one assumes a nonchalant posture toward morality, disaster is not likely to take place immediately. The promiscuous young woman may appear to have an advantage over the virtuous girl. If she's adept at attracting men, she may even have them competing for her affection. On the other hand, the Christian single girl may find herself sitting alone at home listening to the stereo and reading books on Saturday nights. Neither one of these people may understand that what happens on Saturday night isn't the end of the story. Persistent sin eventually catches up with the sinner.

Moses reminded the ancient people of Israel, "You may be sure that your sin will find you out" (Numbers 32:23). All unforgiven sin will be brought to light in eternity. In the case of sexual promiscuity, we're beginning to learn that there's often a high price to pay for the so-called sexual freedom of our times. Genital herpes and AIDS have already rendered irreparable damage to many lives. The suffering in this life can be quite traumatic, and in the case of AIDS, eternity moves closer.

Why We Need a Savior

We need a Savior because only Jesus is qualified to deliver us from the power and the penalty of sin. Peter had no qualms about telling the people responsible for the crucifixion of Jesus that their only hope lay in Christ. He said, "Salvation is found in no one else, for there is no other name under heaven given to men by which we must be saved" (Acts 4:12). Since we are all guilty of sin, and since Jesus is the only Savior, we're led to the inescapable conclusion that we must come under His control or suffer the penalty of death that Paul described in Romans 6:23.

The permissiveness of our times has lulled us into thinking that sin really isn't much of a problem.

> A popular country and western song from the fairly recent past reveals the musings of a man who admits to hanging out in bars and cheating on his wife. He's galled by the intrusion of a certain Mrs. Johnson, whom he looks upon as a self-righteous person out slumming. While conceding the immorality of his behavior, he insists that he will fix everything up with the good Lord in his bedtime prayers.

The singer knows he's out of line in terms of responsible deportment, but he figures he can get away with it. He sees God as a sort of celestial good ole boy who really doesn't take these matters all that seriously—provided the sinner will fix things up with a short bedtime prayer. Such a romanticized view of God, combined with a trivialized understanding of sin, ignores the magnitude of sin's nature and the extent of its consequences. Sin can wrench us from the arms of a loving God! Only a Savior can deliver us from the awful penalty and enslaving power of sin.

> Dark is the stain that
>   We cannot hide.
> What can avail to wash it away?
> Look, there is a flowing,
>   A crimson tide.
> Whiter than snow
>   You may be today.
> —Anonymous

The Bible uses three expressions to describe what Jesus does in helping us with the sin problem.

1. *He enables us to receive forgiveness.* W. E. Vine suggests that the word *forgive* involves two different actions that have taken place in the mind of God. First, the sinner is delivered from the penalty of sin; second, the cause of alienation between God and man is removed.[2] John reminds us, "If we confess our sins, he is faithful and just to forgive us our sins, and to cleanse us from all unrighteousness" (1 John 1:9, KJV).

2. *He makes sure our sins are wiped out.* Peter said, "Repent, then, and turn to God, so that your sins may be wiped out" (Acts 3:19). The ancient people wrote on papyrus with ink made from charcoal mixed with gum and oil. They usually corrected mistakes by writing a large X through them. The X was the Greek letter X. There were times, however, when scribes would start all over

by washing the ink off the paper so that the text would be completely obliterated. In describing what happens to a person who repents and turns, Peter used the word suggesting that sin has been so completely obliterated that it is as if it had never happened.[3]

3. *He washes sins away.* Ananias told Paul, "And now what are you waiting for? Get up, be baptized and wash your sins away, calling on [the name of the Lord]" (Acts 22:16). In Acts 3:19, the emphasis is on removal; in Acts 22:16, it is on being made clean. The prophet Isaiah felt the burden of uncleanness when he looked into the throne room of God, and he said, "I am a man of unclean lips, and I live among a people of unclean lips" (Isaiah 6:5). Our Savior removes the stain of uncleanness when penitent believers are baptized into Christ. William Cowper eloquently expressed the concept of Acts 22:16 when he wrote,

> There is a fountain filled with blood
> Drawn from Immanuel's veins:
> And sinners, plunged beneath that flood,
> Lose all their guilty stains.

Summary and Conclusion

To understand our need for a Savior, we must recognize our vulnerable condition. As members of the human race, we have been victimized by a malignant and destructive force known as sin. Even though the problem of sin is universal, we develop ingenious ways of trying to avoid it. Some try denying the existence of sin. Others rationalize their behavior. Some admit their guilt, but then delay dealing with it. Another avoidance technique involves pretending perfection while ignoring symptoms of sinful attitudes.

Attempts to avoid the reality of sin deceive people and lull them into a false sense of security. People need genuine security, which requires a willingness to accept the fact that sin has produced alienation from God.

In contrast to that unhappy state of affairs, Christ as our Savior promises remission of sins, a release from indebtedness to sin, forgiveness, deliverance from the penalty of sin, and removal of one's alienation from God. Because our sins are obliterated from God's records, we are able to stand in a purified condition before our Creator. No accountable person is exempt from sin, thus no accountable person can claim he doesn't need a Savior.

Thought Questions

1. How can we best help a person understand his need for a Savior if he is not familiar with the Christian vocabulary?
2. Identify different ways human experience confirms the reality of sin.
3. Why do so many people deny the existence of sin?
4. Can you think of any warning signals that indicate we might be attempting to rationalize sin?
5. Why do some people try to deal with the sin problem by pretending perfection?
6. How does sin deprive us of personal freedom?
7. How is it possible to be free and observe restrictions on our behavior at the same time?
8. What are the practical implications of having sins wiped out?

9. Why do people long for spiritual cleanliness?

Notes

[1]Dietrich Bonhoeffer, *Spiritual Care,* trans. Jay C. Rochelle (Philadelphia: Fortress Press, 1985), p. 31.

[2]W. E. Vine, *Expository Dictionary of New Testament Words* (Old Tappan, N.J.: Fleming H. Revell, 1966), II: 122-23.

[3]Roger Johnson, "The Mercy Which Wipes Out Sin," *Sharpstown Sound,* Houston, TX (November 19, 1980).

God Is So Good

God is so good.
God is so good.
God is so good.
He's so good to me.

Seated on logs padded only by thin blankets, young people stare at the leaping flames of roaring campfires and blend their voices in unison as they sing about God's goodness. Against the backdrop of starlit skies and towering trees, the theme of God's care for His people echoes into the cool night air at summer youth camps across the country. How much these young people grasp of what they're singing, I'm not prepared to say. Nevertheless, they're affirming a belief in a benevolent God. Their belief song implies that

- God knows what's going on in the world.
- He cares about what happens to people.
- He is willing to help people.
- He is powerful enough to do what He wants to accomplish.

Biblical writers commit themselves to the premise that God is good and that He holds the ultimate power in the universe. He is frustrated neither by human opposition to His purposes nor by satanic deviousness. He is capable of doing "immeasurably more than all we ask or imagine, according to his power that is at work within us" (Ephesians 3:20).

The young people at our summer camps have temporarily retreated from the harshness of a violent, hostile world. In the relative security of a Christian environment, they may find it easy to focus on God's goodness. Away from those tall trees and on the asphalt streets of our cities and towns, they live in a world plagued by substandard housing, child and spouse abuse, disease, pornography, screaming sirens, racism, drug dealing, car bombings, starvation, and every form of human cruelty the twisted minds of perverted men can invent. In that world, it's not quite so easy to sing with confidence, "God is so good."

The secular humanists have given up on the concept of a good God who makes things happen in the modern world. To them, faith in a prayer-hearing God can be asserted only by those who are naive and uninformed.

> As in 1933, humanists still believe that traditional theism, especially faith in the prayer hearing god, assumed to love and care for persons, to hear and understand their prayers, and to be able to do something about them is an unproved and outmoded faith. Salvationism based on mere affirmation still appears as harmful, diverting people with false hopes of heaven hereafter. Reasonable minds look to other means for survival.[1]

From the opposite end of the spectrum, a Christian often feels the pressure of a God who sounds tyrannical and despotic as He is explained from the pulpit and in the classroom. God has all kinds of power, but He is not very kind according to some who want to provide instruction on the subject. J. B. Phillips says He is like a "resident policeman . . . and overexacting tyrant."[2]

Christians in the twentieth century haven't pursued the study of God's nature with the same vigor they've shown with regard to other topics. If you go to a Christian bookstore, you won't find many serious works devoted to the massive subject of defining God's nature. It's understandable that scholars approach the subject with fear and trembling. After all, there is no more ponderous subject matter in the entire discipline of human inquiry. If you feel inadequate to grapple with the study of God, you're in good company. The apostles and prophets encountered the same reluctance.

But does the problem of tackling the topic of God's nature stem from our humility or our superficiality? Could it be that book publishers don't encourage our intellectual heavyweights to write on the subject because they know such books are likely to gather dust on the shelves? Perhaps the religious book-buying public prefers glib answers, catchphrases, and slogans to substantial theology. Some people regard the term *theology* as a negative word. But it simply means "the study of God."

We can't afford the luxury of hanging on to superficial concepts of God. The insecurity in the hearts of uneasy Christians demands that we more carefully define God's nature and that we come to grips with God's goodness. Short answers won't do. Clever analogies usually break down. We must bring people to an awareness of the biblical concept of God.

British theologian J. I. Packer has broken out of the mold of catchphrase theology and attempted to write a definitive work on the nature of God. In his introduction,

Packer exposes his vulnerability: "As a clown yearns to play Hamlet, so I have wanted to write a treatise on God."[3] I have no illusion, either, about my ability to perform lines from Shakespeare or my capacity to explain the nature of Deity. Nevertheless, I'm confronted with the awareness that grace can never be properly explained until we eliminate some of the commonly believed erroneous ideas about God. Packer laments the confusion that abounds in the popular mind:

> Modern muddle-headedness and confusion as to the meaning of faith in God is almost beyond description. Men say they believe in God, but they have no idea who it is they believe in or what difference believing in Him may make.[4]

An Affirmation of God's Goodness

Both Old and New Testaments agree that God is good. Theologians sometimes portray Yahweh in the Old Testament as an angry God who always has His foot on somebody's neck, while the New Testament version of God is presented in loving, compassionate terms. Of course, it's possible to do just that if one picks and chooses at random from the biblical descriptions of God. It's very easy to line up a whole series of stories to confirm one's theory. The expulsion of Adam and Eve from the Garden of Eden, the destruction of the earth by flood, the death sentence pronounced on every Israelite above the age of twenty with the exception of Joshua and Caleb, the death of Uzzah, and the violent demise of the children who made fun of Elisha's bald head can all be used to confirm the theory that the Old Testament God is unbendingly harsh.

Although retribution is clearly a part of the Old Testament picture, an objective portrait can't be completed unless one is willing to "consider therefore the *kindness* and sternness of God" (Romans 11:22, emphasis added). When Moses needed reassurance from God, he pleaded, "Now show me your glory" (Exodus 33:18). Instead of responding with some kind of awesome display of His firepower, God answered, "I will cause all my *goodness* to pass in front of you" (Exodus 33:19, emphasis added).

The Psalms abound in references to God's kind and benevolent nature. No portion of the Bible speaks more explicitly concerning God's relationship with the human race than Psalm 103:11-14:

> For as high as the heavens are above the earth,
>   so great is his love for those who fear him;
> as far as the east is from the west,
>   so far has he removed our transgressions from us.
> As a father has compassion on his children,
>   so the LORD has compassion on those who fear him;
> for he knows how we are formed,
>   he remembers that we are dust.

It's difficult to think of an Old Testament prophet without forming a mental picture of a man with a burr under his saddle. The prophets are indeed a group of hard-liners. Their repertoire includes woes, complaints, and dire predictions of disaster, but the Bible student who sees only the negative side of their message will overlook their tenderness. Who can not be touched by the magnanimous love of Hosea, the compassionate weeping of Jeremiah, and the optimism of Ezekiel in his story about the valley of dry bones? In one of the most bitter and sorrowful books of the Old Testament, the prophet Jeremiah delivered these upbeat thoughts:

> Because of the LORD's great love we are not consumed,
>   for his compassions never fail.
> They are new every morning;
>   great is your faithfulness.
> I say to myself, "The LORD is my portion;
>   therefore I will wait for him" (Lamentations 3:22-24).

The New Testament echoes the same theme. When the rich young ruler talked to Jesus about good things, Jesus saw it as an opportunity to instruct him about God's nature. He said, "Why do you ask me about what is good? . . . There is only One who is good" (Matthew 19:17). Paul asked the Jews who had wrongly assessed their own spiritual condition, "Do you show contempt for the riches of his kindness, tolerance and patience, not realizing that God's *kindness* leads you toward repentance?" (Romans 2:4, emphasis added). The twentieth-century church needs to reflect on Paul's view of behavior modification. He bypasses the opportunity to use manipulative rhetoric; cheap-shot artists do that. Paul said that God's kindness causes people to repent.

John wrote to a church troubled by teachers who had a twisted view of spirituality. A sophisticated brand of rhetoric had developed in which some Christians were made to feel inferior because they weren't considered to have the same knowledge level as the professed elite members. John cut through the Gordian knot of confusion by concentrating on the loving nature of God: "And so we know and rely on the love God has for us. God is love" (1 John 4:16).

Inadequate Concepts of Love

Have Christians invented their own God? The atheists say that has happened, but the facts indicate a different conclusion. Paul declared, "For since the creation of the world God's invisible qualities—his eternal power and divine nature—have been clearly seen, being understood from what has been made, so that men are without excuse" (Romans 1:20).

Although the existence of God can't be dismissed as a mere invention of man, we are nonetheless forced to admit that some people have developed their own ideas about God more from tradition and wishful thinking than from the revelation of Holy Scripture. There's so much of the muddle-headedness Packer speaks about that fanciful interpretations of God's nature may well lead the list of doctrinal errors. It's beyond the scope of this work to discuss all the views of God's nature, but there are two humanly invented concepts that are especially harmful to the biblical picture of grace.

The first one is that of viewing our Creator as a *ceremonial god*. Ceremonialists differ from one another concerning which ceremonies God will and will not honor. They do share the belief that God bestows His favor on the human race in response to the offering of certain worship structures, liturgies, and rites.

The ceremonial god lives in the heart of the motorist who displays a St. Christopher statue on his dashboard. He is convinced that the plastic image will ensure his protection from accidents, even though it might partially block his vision. Others are confident that counting beads, repeating specific chants, and venerating favorite saints will earn them special favor from God. One's lifestyle may be a contradiction of biblical morality, but that's counterbalanced by correct ritual performance.

A different kind of ceremonialist rejects the statues, the rosaries, and the long-standing religious traditions, but still attaches supreme importance to correct structure as a measurement of faithfulness. When the issue of multiple containers takes on such significance that the cup in which the fruit of the vine is served determines the validity of one's discipleship, does it not suggest that a person has bought into the ceremonial concept of God? When people argue others into the ground over the exact words to be spoken over a baptismal candidate, correct observance of ceremony overshadows the divine purpose for baptism. Some people emphasize doctrinal correctness concerning the proper form of baptism, the use of instruments in the worship, the frequency of observing the Lord's Supper, and other ceremonial aspects of serving God without giving much attention to moral behavior, loving attitudes, and servanthood. To be sure, New Testament patterns do exist and must be respected. Nevertheless, when matters of ceremony become the major tenets of religion, we must remember that Jesus came down hard on the Pharisees who meticulously tithed of their garden vegetables, but then "neglected the more important matters of the law—justice, mercy, and faithfulness" (Matthew 23:23).

Translating Christianity into the experience of daily living doesn't seem to cross the minds of some church members. Religious security systems have been developed in which doctrinal correctness and right ritual become the only considerations for measuring faithfulness. I'm not suggesting that we relax our concern for doctrinal precision. I'm not implying that the church should forget about restoring New Testament patterns of worship. On the other hand, when we see those areas as the primary focus of our energy, we have seriously misunderstood the nature of God and how favor from Him is received. Apparently some of the people who lived in Isaiah's day made this same mistake. They worked hard at being ceremonially correct, but their hearts weren't moved with compassion for others. God said to them,

> Stop bringing meaningless offerings!
>   Your incense is detestable to me.
> New Moons, Sabbaths and convocations—
>   I cannot bear your evil assemblies (Isaiah 1:13).

Another popular concept of God might be labeled the *health-and-wealth god.* Some of the religious media figures actively promote this man-made god. God is viewed as a sort of heavenly Daddy Warbucks. The downtrodden people of the earth are trudging along through life facing all the trials that complicate and trouble the lives of Little Orphan Annie and her faithful dog, Sandy. Then just at the precise moment when it appears that all hope for rescue has disappeared, God steps in like Daddy Warbucks to rescue His children from peril, and lavishes them with bulging bank accounts and healthy bodies.

According to the media version of God, an unlimited supply of material resources can be acquired through appropriate expressions of faith. Of course, the best way to exhibit faith is to prime the pump with a little seed money. The media figures are anxious to point out their presumption that God temporarily receives mail at their addresses and holds His funds in their bank accounts.

The health-and-wealth god looks attractive to people who are wearied with the trauma of burden bearing. They're tired of constantly experiencing the agony of defeat without ever knowing the thrill of victory. Their cares shouldn't be regarded lightly. Often their suffering is so acute and intense that they are understandably willing to reach out to anyone who offers a panacea. But what happens when they realize the unpleasant truth that there is no pot of gold at the end of the rainbow—when the panacea turns out to be a placebo? When sufferers discover the truth about the slick-talking preacher—that he is a medicine man with a bottle of snake oil in one hand and a Bible in the other—can they not become disillusioned with the idea of God altogether?

If it's true that God wants us to go through life with no financial problems and if He wants us to be delivered from every disease, starting with headaches and moving all the way through cancer, then how do we explain the suffering of a devout man like Job? Indeed, how do we explain Paul's perspective in 2 Corinthians 4:8-9? He said, "We are hard pressed on every side, but not crushed; perplexed, but not in despair; persecuted, but not abandoned; struck down, but not destroyed." He also stated, "For your sake we face death all day long; we are considered as sheep to be slaughtered" (Romans 8:36). God has not left us adrift in the world without help for our earthly problems, but the fact is, God's goodness doesn't suggest that He will always shield Christians from adversity.

The Biblical View of God's Goodness

If we believe in God's goodness, we must also be willing

to affirm that He is *just.* Otherwise, grace becomes nothing more than superficial Sunday school sentimentalism. Some people seem to work from the premise suggesting that God wants people to live right, but then if they don't behave, everything will still be all right because grace covers all sin. That kind of theology doesn't take into consideration the fact that God is just.

Because of this aspect of His nature, God requires repentance. At the household of Cornelius, Peter said, "I now realize how true it is that God does not show favoritism but accepts men from every nation who fear him and do what is right" (Acts 10:34-35). Doing what is right must become the aspiration of every person who seeks God's favor. People living in a permissive culture must not lose sight of that significant goal. The loving and merciful God who is so willing to forgive sin has no tolerance for sin. It's at variance with His nature, as evidenced by Habakkuk's statement to the Lord, "Your eyes are too pure to look on evil" (1:13).

An honest evaluation of our own attitude toward sin can expose a deeper awareness of God's righteousness. When Isaiah was confronted with God's glory, he was overwhelmed by his own inadequacy. He cried, "Woe to me! . . . I am ruined! For I am a man of unclean lips, and I live among a people of unclean lips, and my eyes have seen the King, the LORD Almighty" (Isaiah 6:5). When Isaiah came into God's presence, his comprehension of God's righteousness left him totally devastated. Too often the modern worshiper comes into the presence of a just and holy God and goes away complaining of boredom.

> Many of our worship assemblies are not character-
> ized by preparation of heart, the framework of
> reference in which our attitudes are attuned to the
> sacred privilege of seeking God in public assembly.
> Some are gum chewers, clock watchers, interested
> critics or peaceful spectators . . . two extremes may
> be noted in terms of worship procedures. At one
> pole are the noise and confusion, the backslapping
> familiarity of the disorganized service. At the other
> end is the mechanical, perfunctory performance of
> people who seek formality and who are very much
> in a hurry.[5]

Even though God must be viewed as a sovereign and
just Deity, we must not consider Him a cruel despot.
At Sinai, the Lord spoke of His sense of balance: "The
LORD, the LORD, the compassionate and gracious God,
slow to anger, abounding in love and faithfulness, main-
taining love to thousands, and forgiving wickedness,
rebellion and sin. Yet he does not leave the guilty
unpunished" (Exodus 34:6-7).

From our perspective, the most important facet of
God's goodness involves His intervention in the history
of the world to forgive fallen people: "The Lord is not
slow in keeping his promise, as some understand slowness.
He is patient with you, not wanting anyone to perish,
but everyone to come to repentance" (2 Peter 3:9).
God's determination to rescue members of the human
race from the path of self-destruction overrides every
other concern. Sometimes we forget that. We so despise
the sin corrupting our world—the practice of homosexual-
ity, child and spouse abuse, racism, sexual promiscuous-
ness, substance abuse, terrorism—that we may forget how
God sees the people who have been victimized by sin.
He sees them through loving eyes and longs to forgive

them. His outrage is directed toward the sin that has shattered their personhood, not toward the people themselves.

As forgiven sinners, we must be careful in our approach to those who haven't yet escaped the entanglements of sin. There is no way to bring the sinner under the protective umbrella of God's grace without confrontation, but it must be done carefully. Confronting the sinner is a little bit like raising African violets. If you give African violets too much light at one time, you'll destroy them. We must learn how to tear down the sinner's defense mechanisms while leaving his self-esteem intact. That's particularly tricky when the sinner doesn't have much self-esteem to begin with. Confrontation has to be handled with compassion. To some Christians, compassion sounds like soft soap. Perhaps we'll be encouraged to find that delicate sense of balance if we'll remember that God's primary interest in people is saving them, not condemning them.

Summary and Conclusion

We live in a world where a secularist mind-set downplays belief in a powerful and good God. That mind-set affects everyday living in that we feel pressured to behave as if we were all alone in the world, entirely dependent on our own resources for survival. While the Christian is being pressured by humanism on one side, he may well feel the tightening vise from the opposite direction when well-meaning religious teachers use the threat of God's disapproval to satisfy their own subconscious power urges.

Although some theologians have tried to portray God as a rather inconsistent heavenly being by depicting

Him as a fire-breathing adversary in the Old Testament and as a loving friend in the New Testament, no such dichotomy actually exists. Both Testaments insist that He is just, but humanly invented concepts of God have distorted these biblical portrayals. An accurate assessment of God, as He is described in the biblical record, will bring us to the realization that the God whose eyes are too pure to look on evil has an intense desire to bring fallen men and women into union with Him.

> There are questions for which we have only partial answers. However, there are also certainties upon which we can depend. Nothing is more certain than God's love. Similarly, the evidence of God's love is overwhelming. God's way is the best way. It is the most reasonable way. Ultimately, it is the only way.[6]

Thought Questions

1. Why do so many people in today's world challenge the premise that God is both powerful and merciful?
2. Why do you think there is such a dearth of published material by Christian thinkers on the nature of God?
3. How do you respond to the commonly held belief that the Old Testament presents a God of severity and the New Testament presents a God of love?
4. Why is the ceremonial god so attractive to people?
5. Consider the comparison between certain human concepts of God and the Daddy Warbucks character in the "Little Orphan Annie" comic strip series.

6. In rejecting the health-and-wealth god, is it still possible to credit God for material prosperity and good health?
7. What additional humanly devised concepts of God distort the biblical description of God?
8. Why does God's sense of justice necessarily include His willingness to forgive sin?
9. Why do Christians approach a just and holy God in a spirit of casualness?
10. How can we avoid the extremes of permissiveness and judgmentalism in our relationships with people whose lives have been damaged by sin?

Notes

[1]"Humanist Manifesto II," *The Humanist,* September-October 1973.

[2]J. B. Phillips, *Your God Is Too Small* (New York: Macmillan, 1961), p. 15.

[3]J. I. Packer, *Knowing God* (Downers Grove, Ill.: Intervarsity Press, 1973), p. 5.

[4]Ibid., p. 143.

[5]Jack Bates, "The Holiness of God," in *Abilene Christian College Bible Lectures 1958,* ed. J. D. Thomas (Austin, Tex.: Firm Foundation Publishing House, 1958), p. 278.

[6]Batsell Barrett Baxter, *I Believe Because* (Grand Rapids, Mich.: Baker Book House, 1971), p. 278.

C H A P T E R   3

The Clash Between Justice and Mercy

In our modern world, the ideas and trends that gain widespread acceptance among the rank and file are often called *pop*. Vogue terms include pop music, pop art, the pop culture, and even pop psychology. There is also an area of pop religion. C. S. Lewis offers a unique description of this phenomenon: "It is the view I call Christianity-and-water. The view that simply says there is a good God in heaven and everything is all right—leaving out the difficult and terrible doctrines about sin and hell and the devil and the redemption."[1] J. I. Packer believes this Santa Claus theology has become the dominant current in popular thinking: "To reject all ideas of divine wrath and judgment and to assume that God's character . . . is really one of indulgent benevolence without any severity, is the rule rather than the exception among ordinary folks today."[2]

U.S. Catholic magazine conducted a survey on religious attitudes in America and reported that 93 percent of the respondents believed in the existence of heaven. Even though 86 percent of those answering the questions believed in the existence of hell, only 22 percent were willing to say they thought Hitler might be in hell, and a mere 10 percent selected Judas for eternal condemnation.[3]

Wishful Thinking

Perhaps the most identifiable characteristic of pop religion is its preoccupation with wishful thinking. An old folk song tells about a bum who wished for the "lemonade springs where the bluebird sings in the big rock candy mountain." Shakespeare immortalized the desperate king who longed for "a horse, a horse. My kingdom for a horse."[4]

Some people seem to live for those kinds of wishes. The farmer wishes he had better weather. The investor wishes for a more favorable market, and the diehard Cub fans wish for another year like 1984. For the most part, these wishes are harmless mental exercises that temporarily take our minds away from our daily troubles.

Wishes can be damaging, however. The expression *wishful thinking* comes from the world of psychology and is defined as "thinking of a thing to be true because one wants it to be true."[5] Sometimes people form their attitudes toward life and select their behavior patterns on the basis of what they wish to be true.

Racists believe they are justified in treating other people as inferiors because they don't wish God to treat other people with equal regard. Covetous persons defend their greed because in their own twisted version of wishful thinking, God has chosen them for special favors. Adherents to various systems of religion and philosophy refuse to engage in any kind of meaningful truth search because they desire the ideas handed down to them from previous generations to be true.

The pop religion approach, which is so often rooted in wishful thinking, doesn't take into consideration a basic premise of logic suggesting that truth is noncontradictory. As it is sometimes stated, A cannot be non-A.

We must keep this in mind as we consider salvation by grace. God's mercy must be made available to the human race in ways that are consistent with His sense of justice. In Romans 3, Paul establishes the fact that the human race has justly come under the indictment of sin (3:9). As guilty sinners, we therefore deserve condemnation (Romans 1:32, 2:2, 5).

The gospel comes to us as good news from God, because through it we learn that God has intervened in our lives in such a way as to treat us as righteous people (Romans 3:21). This intervention has the practical effect of bringing forgiveness to undeserving sinners and at the same time satisfying all the requirements of divine justice: "He did it to demonstrate his justice at the present time, so as to be just and the one who justifies those who have faith in Jesus" (Romans 3:26).

Why Must God Be Just?

A person who believes that "God's in his heaven—All's right with the world" has great difficulty understanding why God had to go through the painful process of sending His Son to die on the cross. The sinner who has been brought under conviction wants God to do something about his sin problem, but he doesn't really worry all that much about satisfying the demands of divine justice. While the clash between the concepts of justice and mercy is far too complex to be fully comprehended by any mere mortal, we must at least understand that God can't extend grace unless He is also just.

He must be just because He governs the universe by certain irrevocable laws. We all expect God's physical laws to remain constant. Life would be a terrible ordeal if God were to suspend the laws of motion and inertia about every third day. Can you image what kind of frustration we would experience if God changed the temperature for the boiling point every day? Our lives would be completely chaotic if God should choose to alter the number of hours for daylight and the number of hours for darkness according to His daily whims.

The adherents of pop religion don't realize that God is bound to consistency in the realm of moral law. When Adam and Eve were given the run of the garden, consistent moral law prevailed. They were clearly told, "You must not eat from the tree of the knowledge of good and evil, for when you eat of it you will surely die" (Genesis 2:17). When they violated that law, God was thus obligated to follow up with the predicted consequence. Had He not done so, our relationship with Him would be as unpredictable as the relationship the ancient pagan people imagined they had with their numerous deities.

In Abraham's attempt to persuade God to change His mind about destroying Sodom, the patriarch indicated an understanding of this essential aspect of God's nature. He said, "Will you sweep away the righteous with the wicked? What if there are fifty righteous people in the city? . . . Far be it from you to do such a thing—to kill the righteous with the wicked . . . Will not the Judge of all the earth do right?" (Genesis 18:23-25). Abraham failed to realize that the entire population of Sodom didn't even come close to including fifty righteous people, but his understanding of God's sense of justice was right on target. God doesn't treat the righteous and the wicked the same way. He blesses the righteous and punishes the wicked.

Lest we fall into the trap of thinking that retribution belongs solely to the rigidity of the Old Testament period, we must remember that Paul said, "Do not be deceived: God cannot be mocked. A man reaps what he sows. The one who sows to please his sinful nature, from that nature will reap destruction; the one who sows to please the Spirit, from the Spirit will reap eternal life" (Galatians 6:7-8). Clearly, God's sense of justice includes the necessity of retribution. The grace-faith system doesn't repeal Judgment Day! As Paul wrote, "For we must all appear before the judgment seat of Christ, that each one may receive what is due him for the things done while in the body, whether good or bad" (2 Corinthians 5:10).

That's why pop religion comes up short. When we drink the heady wine of material prosperity, we become intoxicated with the same false sense of well-being that an alcoholic experiences when he has consumed his favorite spirit. Because we've managed to live in a world where a high level of technological advancement has made it possible for us to enjoy all kinds of creature comforts from sophisticated music systems to air conditioning, we may have developed a tendency to believe that our comfort and our sense of cultured sophistication have come to us because we are looked upon as God's favorite sons and daughters.

It's easy to believe in the God who patronizes His greedy children when life's most complex problem comes down to making a choice between speakers for a new stereo system. But pop religion won't play among the starving people of the Third World. Don't try to sell it to the husband who's watching his wife slowly waste away under the assault of an inoperable tumor. Pop religion doesn't serve very well the mother who watched her child dart into the path of an oncoming car and now repeatedly replays the sound of screeching brakes and the thud of tires that snuffed out the life of her precious offspring.

When those tragedies take place, pop religionists are forced to reevaluate their view of God. They must reject God, conclude that God's power is limited, or revise their perception of God. Packer describes the frustration of the person who tries to hold on to the pop religion version of God:

> Thus he is left with a kind of God who means well, but cannot always insulate his children against trouble and grief. When trouble comes, there is nothing to do but grin and bear it. In this way, by an ironic paradox, faith in a God who is all goodness and no severity, tends to confirm men in a fatalistic and pessimistic attitude toward life.[6]

Amnesty Doesn't Solve the Problem

To some people, the only workable solution to the sin problem is that of having God declare a moratorium on all punishment for sin. In chapters 1 and 2, we observed that God is good. He wants to forgive, and forgiveness is most certainly within the range of His power. Paul said He is "able to do immeasurably more than all we ask or imagine, according to his power that is at work within us" (Ephesians 3:20). If God is both good and powerful, then why doesn't He simply declare universal amnesty for the entire human race and be done with the problem?

The concept of amnesty suggests the intentional overlooking of offenses. The word came into popular usage after the war in Vietnam. That Southeast Asian conflict so sharply divided the American people that many thought it would be in the country's best interests to extend universal amnesty to all those young men who had refused induction into the military. Some thought it would heal the bitterness in the country if the government would simply wipe the whole slate clean and forget about the technical violations of the selective service laws.

Although some viewed amnesty as a tolerant and even merciful solution to a thorny problem, others said, "But it's not right." Regardless of one's views about Vietnam, the fact remained that the structure of an orderly society depends on respect for established law. If the draft laws were to become meaningless today, then there would likely be very little respect for the traffic laws tomorrow. People might sneer at the law-and-order concept, but a nation would not survive in the midst of anarchy.

There is a sense in which God confronts the same kind of dilemma. If He offers us amnesty, He runs the risk of dismantling the entire social and moral order. Would we really be satisfied with a God who rewards people like those who planned and carried out the Holocaust? Is Hitler entitled to the same reward as Peter and Paul? How much restraint can we expect people to observe if they are offered an honored place in God's family without the necessity of undergoing character change, without repentance, without atonement, and without satisfying God's requirements in any way? On the other hand, the very best we have to offer God isn't nearly good enough. As Isaiah reminded us, "All our righteous acts are like filthy rags" (Isaiah 64:6).

We need only to look at the Bible to learn how people act when all restraints are dropped. For example, early in the biblical account it is recorded that "the LORD saw how great man's wickedness on the earth had become, and that every inclination of the thoughts of his heart was only evil all the time" (Genesis 6:5). The book of Judges describes another period in which moral laxity prevailed. The reason for such poor behavior patterns is offered in Judges 21:25: "In those days Israel had no king; everyone did as he saw fit."

Why We Can't Govern Ourselves

How do we account for this inability of people to behave responsibly? Philosophers and theologians have offered various explanations about what makes the human being tick. At one end of the spectrum, the Calvinists say that we are victims of the sin nature that has been passed down from our original parents who got things off to a pretty bad start in the Garden of Eden. They conclude that "man's nature is corrupt, perverse and sinful throughout."[7] They are convinced that we came into this world "totally unable to do anything spiritually good."[8]

At the opposite end of the spectrum, one may point to the nineteenth-century liberal theologians who don't believe anything to be radically wrong with human nature. They manage to purge all the guilt from sinful man by the simple act of declaring him free from the taint of sin and by depicting sin as a manipulative tool of a power hungry religious class. They insist, "There is no sharp cleavage between God and man, for man at his best is like God. Man can be won from sin by education and by holding before him the ideas of Jesus."[9]

The radical optimism of those nineteenth-century idealists was shattered when World War I erupted on the European continent in 1914. The events of the twentieth century have subsequently shown that education by itself does not make men better. Theodore Roosevelt once said, "A man without an education may rob a train, but an educated man without principles will steal a railroad." One shudders to remember that some of the men who operated the death camps during the Holocaust were family men who listened to concerts featuring the music of Beethoven and Bach during their free time.

The Calvinist explanation lacks both biblical and logical support. According to Scripture, "The soul who sins is the one who will die. The son will not share the guilt of the father, nor will the father share the guilt of the son" (Ezekiel 18:20). If the Calvinists' explanation of the sin nature be correct, we would logically conclude that biblical commands mandating responsible behavior can be understood by anyone except regenerate people. Yet we all know unsaved people who are capable of great humanitarian gestures and who display a high degree of moral integrity.

A better solution is suggested by those who believe the human race has been created with the capacity to choose. The responsibility for guilt then falls on the shoulders of the person who commits sin. We're not held accountable for sins committed by others who lived long before our time. The Bible explicitly states that we have all chosen the pathway of sin (Romans 3:23), but nowhere does it suggest that we are born with some kind of curse imbedded into our nature. We sin because we choose to sin. The history of the human race indicates that sin increases in frequency and in audacity when people believe they will not be held accountable for the things they do.

God Wants to Bring Healing

The sin problem has damaged us severely; without God's help, we are extremely vulnerable to the deceitful devices of Satan. However, God has provided "protective" armor to help us resist the devil's attacks. Of course, the armor can aid us only if we choose to put it on, and that choice always remains with us. But if we elect to "put on the full armor of God," we are promised the ability to "stand against the devil's schemes" (Ephesians 6:11).

Unfortunately, some Christians have learned the lesson about God's retribution quite well, but they haven't seen the compassionate side of the Father's nature. Paul urged us to "consider therefore the kindness and sternness of God" (Romans 11:22). Those who long for amnesty have fixated on God's kindness and dismissed His sternness. That's a mistake, but it's no more serious than the mistake of focusing on God's sternness while ignoring His kindness.

God's main business with the human race is salvation, not condemnation: "He is patient with you, not wanting anything to perish" (2 Peter 3:9). That is why John 3:16 has become a favorite verse for so many people. It speaks of God's compassionate attitude toward us and of the great lengths to which He has gone to allow a relationship of harmony to exist between the created one and the

Creator: "For God so loved the world that he gave his one and only Son, that whoever believes in him shall not perish but have eternal life."

Retribution isn't the theme of the Bible story. Salvation is the ultimate truth. That's why the story of Jesus is called *good news*. The entire reason for the Bible, for Christ and the church, and for the whole Christian system is bound up in the message of redemption. John R. W. Stott points out how God's redemption program operates at three different levels:

> Phase one is our deliverance from the guilt and judgment of our sins . . . together with our reconciliation to God. Phase two is our progressive liberation from the down drag of evil beginning with our birth into the family of God and continuing with our transformation by the Spirit of Christ into the image of Christ. Phase three is our final deliverance from the sin which lingers both in our fallen nature and in our social environment, when on the last day, we shall be invested with a new and glorious body and transferred to a new heaven and a new earth in which righteousness dwells.[10]

Summary and Conclusion

While the sensitive human heart yearns to be forgiven, to be delivered from the enslaving power of sin, and to eventually occupy the eternal home God has promised, the possibility of actually realizing these goals overload the circuits in our brains. It's only possible because Jesus has become "just and the one who justifies those who have faith in [Him]" (Romans 3:26). The mysteries of the Atonement are too deep to be explained by any clever analogy. The thought that God can maintain His just posture by allowing His innocent Son to take the penalty of sin on Himself is almost impossible to comprehend.

In some ways, however, the following illustration may help us to appreciate the appeal of God's merciful love. Imagine that you are a member of the Irish Republican Army. You're a terrorist and an insurrectionist. You hate the British Crown. You're caught plotting against the government and sentenced to ten years at hard labor. But you're also the sole breadwinner for a large family. Without your support, they'll starve.

Enter Prince Charles, heir to the British throne. He is touched by the need of your family. He leaves his royal estate, comes to Ireland, appears at the prison gates, and says to the warden, "Free the terrorist. I'll serve his sentence."

When the ten-year sentence is completed, the Prince is summoned to Buckingham Palace. The Queen has died, and the man who has just completed ten years of penal servitude on your behalf is now King Charles.

What would you do? Would you continue your terrorist activities? Would you remain in a state of rebellion against the Crown? Would you consider it beneath your dignity to honor a king who gave ten years of his life so that you might go free?

All of us were rebels at one time; we were enemies of God. A royal figure left the throne of glory, assumed physical form, and ultimately paid the penalty that justly belonged to us: "While we were still sinners, Christ died for us" (Romans 5:8). Calvary lifted the sentence that once hung so ominously over our heads.

Christ Jesus has now been summoned back to the heavenly courts where He occupies a position at the right hand of God: "Therefore God exalted him to the highest place and gave him the name that is above every name" (Philippians 2:9).

How do you respond to the King who served your sentence? Do you continue in your rebellion? Will you willingly reject His offer of clemency? He has accomplished the task of extending pardon when justice seemed to demand eternal punishment. That's the strongest, highest, and noblest motive for serving, loving, and obeying.

Thought Questions

1. Why must God be just?
2. What would be the possible consequences if God were to reward the wicked and the righteous in equal proportions?
3. How does the American middle-class lifestyle encourage us to overlook God's sense of justice?
4. Why isn't it possible for God to offer amnesty?
5. What are the inherent weaknesses in the Calvinistic solution?
6. How did nineteenth-century liberalism attempt to resolve the clash between justice and mercy?
7. Is man inherently evil? Inherently good? Or does he come into the life experience as a blank page?
8. What is involved in putting on the whole armor of God?
9. How can we help Christians who view God more in terms of sternness than in terms of kindness?

10. Why is the gospel to be thought of as a good news message?

Notes

[1]C. S. Lewis, *Mere Christianity* (1952; reprint, London: Fontana Books, 1966), p. 42.

[2]J. I. Packer, *Knowing God* (Downers Grove, Ill.: Intervarsity Press, 1973), p. 144.

[3]Alan Phipps, "What Some Want in Heaven," (Des Moines, Iowa) *Southside Church of Christ Bulletin*, December 8, 1983).

[4]William Shakespeare, *Richard III*, act 5, scene 4, line 7.

[5]Ivor H. Evans, *Brewer's Dictionary of Phrase and Fable*, centenary ed., rev. (New York: Harper and Row, 1981), p. 1188.

[6]Packer, *Knowing God*, p. 145.

[7]David N. Steele and Curtis C. Thomas, *Romans, An Interpretative Outline* (Philadelphia: Presbyterian and Reformed, 1963), p. 86.

[8]Ibid.

[9]William Hordern, *A Layman's Guide to Protestant Theology* (New York: Macmillan, 1961), p. 86.

[10]John R. W. Stott, *Christ, the Controversialist*, Am. ed. (Downers Grove, Ill.: Intervarsity Press, 1970), p. 109.

Jesus Our Savior

When William Tyndale was working on his New Testament translation, he encountered great difficulty in coming up with a word that would adequately describe the work of Christ on the cross. He ultimately settled for coining a new English word. He merged the terms *at* and *onement* to suggest that through Christ we become one. Thus, we have the word *atonement*.[1]

According to Paul, we've allowed ourselves to become God's enemies (Romans 5:10). Christ's work on our behalf makes it possible for us to undergo such a radical transition of relationship that we cease being enemies and become God's children. The term *atonement* designates that process. Of all the concepts that flow from the subject of grace, the Atonement is perhaps the most complex.

In times past, the topic of the Atonement has been allowed to become grist for the debate mill. Theologians have dreamed up a plethora of theories to explain how the Atonement works. Rather than propose yet another hypothesis to fuel more discussion, I'll admit that much of the concept of the Atonement remains shrouded in mystery. I'm sure God intended it to be so. And Paul conceded the mysterious element: "For the message of the cross is foolishness to those who are perishing, but to us who are being saved it is the power of God"

(1 Corinthians 1:18). William Barclay captures the spirit that serves as a guidepost for our investigation when he writes, "The cross is designed to awaken within us, not theological disputation, but a driving love."[2]

The Prince of Peace

"But now in Christ Jesus you who once were far away have been brought near through the blood of Christ. For he himself is our peace" (Ephesians 2:13-14). With these words, the apostle suggested that peace comes to the individual who has been alienated from God at the price of our Lord's blood. Peace has always been a costly blessing. Today our nation enjoys a somewhat peaceful relationship with Japan and the Federal Republic of Germany, but it has not always been so. The white crosses marking the graves on foreign battlefields remind us that the present-day peace was purchased by the sacrifice of human life. The Scriptures constantly remind us that though we have no money to pay for God's blessings, His gifts to us have been nevertheless obtained at a high price. We have been "bought at a price" (1 Corinthians 6:20), and the church has been "bought with his own blood" (Acts 20:28).

According to Mark 10:45, Jesus gave "his life as a ransom for many." Paul contended that Jesus is qualified to serve as our *mediator* because He "gave himself as a ransom for all men" (1 Timothy 2:6). *Ransom* means to "redeem one through the payment of a price." The Scriptures also speak of Jesus as a *redeemer*: He "gave himself for us to redeem us from all wickedness" (Titus 2:14), and we are "redeemed . . . with the precious blood of Christ, a lamb without blemish and defect" (1 Peter 1:18-19).

All this sounds a little strange to twentieth-century ears because we don't live in an era when sacrificial offerings are commonplace. During biblical times, both the pagans and the Jews offered sacrifices in their devotions. The sight of blood sprinkled on an altar would repulse twentieth-century sensibilities, but it was considered to be the ultimate expression of devotion to deity in the ancient world.

We may not be able to comprehend the feelings of religious intensity that surged through ancient people when they offered ceremonial sacrifices, but we do understand the devotion associated with sacrifice, as illustrated in the following anecdote. A little girl was rescued from a burning house by her mother. The flames came so close that the very hands and arms that shielded the baby from the deadly fire were permanently scarred in the process. As the girl grew older, she became conscious of the fact that her mother's hands and arms didn't look like those of other women. She thought they were ugly. She was so ashamed of her mother's appearance that she didn't want to be seen with her in public. One day the mother told her daughter about the fire. When the daughter realized that her own life had been spared because her mother sacrificed the beauty of her hands and arms, she said, "Mother, you have the most beautiful hands in the world." Her perspective changed when she understood the effect of the sacrifice.

The sacrifice of Jesus on the cross may appear to be a grim account of human violence if we view it purely as a Roman execution. The thought of a spear violating the body of Jesus, penetrating the skin, and ripping into His internal organs may well be repulsive to modern people with a well-cultivated sense of human dignity. But when we understand that the Man who died on the cross secured our own salvation, the act is no longer to be thought of in terms of human cruelty. It becomes the ultimate expression of love, the foundation of our hope and the motive for discipleship. Thus, Paul wrote, "May I never boast except in the cross of our Lord Jesus Christ, through which the world has been crucified to me, and I to the world" (Galatians 6:14).

Propitiation

I was brought up on the King James Version of the Bible. When I was called on to read in Sunday school class, I never wanted to read the verses that talked about *propitiation*. In the first place, I couldn't pronounce it, and in the second place, I didn't understand it. The concept of propitiation is crucial, however, to our understanding of the nature of the Atonement.

Modern translators have toyed with alternate terms and phrases. They've come up with such substitutes as "expiation" (RSV), "atoning sacrifice" (NIV), and "the way our sins are taken away" (NEW EASY TO READ VERSION). There really is no English word or phrase to precisely convey the idea of propitiation.

Even though the English term *propitiation* isn't widely understood by English-speaking people, it remains the most accurate translation of the Greek term *hilasterion*. The word appears in Romans 3:25; Hebrews 9:5; 1 John 2:2; and 4:10; its verb form is found in Luke 18:13 (lit. be propitious) and Hebrews 2:17 (merciful). The English term describes "an objective provision for pity or mercy."

In the biblical context, it "can only mean that our account as sinners, before a holy God is objectively settled."[3]

Some modern scholars refuse to accept the propitiation concept because to them, it reduces God to the level of pagan deities. In Greek mythology, there is the story of Prince Paris who kidnapped Princess Helen and took her off to Troy. Agamemnon, the Greek general, set out with his men in ships to rescue the captured princess, but halfway to Troy, the winds began to blow in the wrong direction. The opposing winds continued for several days, and his voyage to Troy was halted. Agamemnon sent for his daughter and ordered her to be ceremoniously slain in order to appease the wrath of Diana. Agamemnon subscribed to the theory that the gods were jealous beings and thus responded to major sacrifices, especially human ones. Thus, getting a favor from a pagan god meant one had to bribe him.

When we start talking about Jesus as "an objective provision for pity or mercy," some people think we're talking about a capricious deity like the gods of Greek mythology. I recall talking with a group of Protestant clergymen about the Atonement. One elderly gentleman raised his voice in agitated disagreement when I suggested that Jesus had to die before man could be reconciled with God. He asked, "Are you actually suggesting that God must be appeased?" To him, the concept of propitiation simply doesn't mesh with the love and mercy of God.

There are at least two significant differences between the propitiation offered by Christ and the jealous anger of the pagan deities. In the first place, God isn't angry because He is bad tempered and jealous. God is angry because justice, truth, righteousness, and morality have been treated with contempt. Secondly, try to view the fall of man from God's perspective. He has given a directive concerning the tree of knowledge of good and evil. He knows that if people violate His commands, they are hurt themselves. As a deterrent, He attaches a consequence: "For when you eat of it you will surely die" (Genesis 2:17). The Genesis record indicates that Adam and Eve clearly understood both the command and the penalty attached to disobedience.

Suppose God says, "Perhaps I was a bit hasty in setting up such rigid requirements. My judgment was flawed, and my anger got the best of me when I invoked the severe penalty of expulsion from the garden. I'm going to let you off this time, but please don't do it again." Such a compromise erodes our confidence in God as a perfect being.

Actually, in making provision for atonement, God does something that never occurs in pagan thought about deity. He provides the sacrifice to satisfy the requirements of eternal justice. He has sent His Son as the just and the justifier (Romans 3:26).

Many years ago, I had the opportunity to study the book of Romans under Dr. J. D. Thomas, who at that time offered a graduate-level course in that epistle at Abilene Christian College. Dr. Thomas used the following illustration to heighten his students' appreciation for the Atonement. Imagine a destitute mother being arrested for stealing a bottle of milk in order to feed her hungry child. Her crime of theft makes her a law violator. She is subsequently indicted and tried in the criminal justice system. When the prosecuting attorney presents his evidence in court, the judge has no alternative other than to find the poor woman guilty as charged. Because of the mitigating circumstances, the judge imposes the minimum sentence, a five-dollar fine. However, a woman who can't afford to buy a bottle of milk for her starving baby can't even pay such a small fine. The judge is a kind and caring man. But how shall he maintain respect for the law and show mercy to the woman at the same time? He resolves the dilemma by removing his judicial robe, taking five dollars from his wallet, and paying it to the bailiff in satisfaction of the judicial sentence. This frees the woman to go home to her baby. Something like that happened when Jesus went to the cross. We have been indicted for our sins and found guilty as charged. The penalty is death (Romans 6:23), and Jesus has paid the debt.

> Jesus paid it all,
> All to Him I owe;
> Sin had left a crimson stain,
> He washed it white as snow.
> —Elvina M. Hall

The Substitutionary Atonement

In Isaiah 53, the prophet provided his readers with a preview of the substitutionary atonement as he described the suffering servant. The suffering servant becomes involved with the whole human race because "the LORD has laid on him the iniquity of us all" (verse 6). Verse 10 helps us to realize that the Cross was no accident: "Yet it was the LORD's will to crush him and cause him to suffer."

The Hebrew nation had been conditioned to understand the principle of offering sacrifice for sin through the tabernacle worship. To the author of Hebrews, the animal sacrifice program was a "shadow of the good things that are coming" (Hebrews 10:1). The idea of sacrifice remains alive, however, throughout the New Testament. When John the Baptist saw Jesus, he spoke of Him in sacrificial terms: "Look, the Lamb of God, who takes away the sin of the world!" (John 1:29). Paul referred to the substitutionary atonement when he wrote, "God made him who had no sin to be sin for us, so that in him we might become the righteousness of God" (2 Corinthians 5:21).

When Jesus went to the cross, He became a substitute for you and me. The nails driven through his hands and feet should rightfully have been ours. Jesus didn't deserve the pain and the mocking crowd. We did. Hell was our just punishment, but Jesus suffered it for us. That's what Isaiah meant when he said, "He was pierced for our transgressions, he was crushed for our iniquities" (Isaiah 53:5).

Christus Victor

In our modern world, we often close our eyes to the violent struggle for the control of the human will. But the writers of Scripture saw the human heart as a battleground on which the most important war of human history is being fought. Perhaps this verse in Ephesians best sums up their attitude: "For our struggle is not against flesh and blood, but against the rulers, against the authorities, against the powers of this dark world and against the spiritual forces of evil in the heavenly realms" (6:12).

Of all the nasty weapons in Satan's arsenal, the worst is death. Death separates us from our loved ones. Death dashes our hopes and dreams. Death is a satanic tactic arrogantly inflicted on the human race. We shouldn't settle for shallow sentimentalism when we're trying to get a handle on our emotions. Death is not a sweet repose. We must never imagine it to be a friend. Scripture calls it an enemy. It's a terrorist maneuver so menacing that God has acted to abolish it (2 Timothy 1:10).

If your experience with the act of dying has been limited to the melodramatic portrayals of the entertainment media, you're in for a real shock when you see a loved one actually go through the experience. The romanticized version doesn't deal with the unbearable pain experienced by a cancer victim. It can't adequately communicate the spirit of desperation that attacks a relationship about to be torn apart by death. It's an agonizing, helpless experience to stand by and observe the gradual breakdown of body functions and the slow physical deterioration that transforms a once robust body into an emaciated shadow of its former self.

Death is Satan's last hurrah. He is inflicting some of the agony of hell on the victim and his loved ones at a time when both physical and emotional strength are rapidly declining. Maybe it's a desperate attempt to persuade the victim to curse God and die.

I refuse to think of death as a friend. Death is a casualty in the war against evil. The Christian doesn't face death courageously because he has rationalized himself into believing that it is some kind of graduation ceremony to prepare him for heaven. He faces it courageously because he knows that even in this, the archterrorist can't win. The Resurrection will demonstrate the completeness of our victory. As Paul wrote, "Thanks be to God! He gives us the victory through our Lord Jesus Christ" (1 Corinthians 15:56).

In his statement to Timothy, Paul contended that Christ "has destroyed death and has brought life and immortality to light" (2 Timothy 1:10). It's difficult for us to understand how Paul could speak in such terms. After all, the presence of the funeral coach reminds us that the mortality rate for the human race still stands at 100 percent. We have to realize that even though the victory has been assured, the battle is still going on.

Some time ago, I listened to a basketball game on the radio. The game was so lopsided that the outcome was fully determined by the halftime break. Yet the winning team had to play out the last half. The losing coach didn't appear at the winning team's locker room and offer to forfeit the game. Our struggle with Satan is like that.

The book of Revelation was written to assure struggling Christians of the victory that God wants us to claim. There are so many self-professed experts who claim to have an inside track on the content of Revelation that many Christians are a bit reluctant to even consider a study of the book. I usually try to avoid Revelation experts the same way I avoid process servers, bill collectors, and aluminum-siding salesmen. I'm not at all curious about the latest theory on the meaning of 666 in Revelation 13. Even so, there's a message that needs to be discerned by Christians who struggle against the tempter.

A preacher was passing the time of day with the church janitor. To make conversation, he said to the janitor, "Sam, I saw you reading your Bible during your lunch break the other day. What portion were you reading?"

"The book of Revelation" came the reply.

The preacher laughed, knowing that Sam's training in biblical exegesis was far inferior to his own. He said, "Well, Sam, have you settled on an interpretive approach? Who's right about Revelation? The futurists? What do you think about the historical approach? Would you describe yourself as a preterist?"

Sam threw up his hands in a gesture of defense. "Hey, preacher, you're throwing around a bunch of words I don't understand. I'm sure you know a lot more about Revelation than I do. I don't know too much about the identity of the beast and the mother of harlots, but I think it clears up one thing in my mind."

"What's that, Sam?" the preacher asked.

Sam scratched his forehead. "Well, it sort of sounds like the Lord and the devil chose up sides and then got into the awfulest fight you ever heard of. But the Lord won."

Sam might not fare too well in a class on critical exegesis, but he got the point about the message of Revelation. The beast and the false prophet are thrown into the lake of fire along with the devil (Revelation 20:10). Christians are released from the imprisonment of an environment that's terrorized by pain, tears, and death.

An aging Christian once described his fear of the Grim Reaper's inevitable appearance by saying, "I don't want that dirt thrown in my face." Nobody does, but the pain and the dread of that moment are eased by our understanding that death is swallowed up in the ultimate victory of the Resurrection.

> One of the great dominant pictures of the work of Jesus Christ in his life and in his death, both in the New Testament and the thought of the early

church, is the picture of Christ, the Victor, the *Christus Victor* theme as it has been called. This is the idea that in his death and his resurrection, Jesus has finally and utterly defeated the evil demonic powers whose aim is to compass the death and the destruction of men.[5]

Summary and Conclusion

Although the concept of Christ's atoning sacrifice can never be fully comprehended by the human mind, even the person who has had no formal training in logic can sincerely understand the words of the Hebrew writer: "Without shedding of blood is no remission" (Hebrews 9:22, KJV).

The modern sophisticated mind-set rebels against the thought of a bloody sacrifice. Human pride reacts negatively to the suggestion that civilized man needs a sin bearer. Nevertheless, Jesus "bore our sins in his body on the tree, so that we might die to sins and live for righteousness" (1 Peter 2:24).

Many years ago, Charlotte Elliott, a talented young woman with a lovely voice, performed before a large gathering of people in London. When the program was over, a preacher took her aside and said, "Young lady, as I listened to you sing, I thought how much it would help the cause of Christ if your talents were dedicated to his cause. You are as much of a sinner in the sight of God as a drunkard in the ditch, or a prostitute in the red light district. But I'm glad to tell you that the blood of Jesus Christ can cleanse your every sin."

Charlotte was highly offended by the man's blunt

accusations, but the preacher simply said, "I wasn't trying
to offend. I just pray that God's spirit will convict you."

The singer went home, but she couldn't sleep. Finally
at two o'clock in the morning, she arose from her bed,
and through her tears, she wrote these words that have
blessed the singers of Christian hymns in all the years
that have followed:

> Just as I am, without one plea,
> But that thy blood was shed for me,
> And that thou bidst me come to thee,
> O lamb of God, I come, I come.
>
> Just as I am, And waiting not
> To rid my soul of one dark blot.
> To thee whose blood can cleanse each spot
> O lamb of God, I come, I come.[6]

Thought Questions

1. What is the meaning of *atonement?*
2. Why does theological debate often miss the intent
   of the Atonement?
3. How does the word *ransom* help us to appreciate
   the work of Christ on the cross?
4. What is the meaning of the term *propitiation?*
5. Why do such expressions, as *expiation* and *atoning
   sacrifice* fall short in communicating the Atonement
   concept to our minds?
6. Why does a sacrifice for our sins have to be made?
7. What is the difference between the propitiation
   offered by Christ and the jealous anger of the pagan
   deities?

8. How do we know the Cross was something more than a poorly managed and unjust execution?
9. Why does the Christian view death as an enemy?
10. Explain the *Christus Victor* theme.

Notes

[1]Billy Graham, *World Aflame* (New York: Doubleday, 1965; Pocket Cardinal Edition, 1966), pp. 100-101.

[2]William Barclay, *Crucified and Crowned* (London: SCM Press, 1961), p. 91.

[3]*Zondervan Pictorial Bible Dictionary*, 1963 ed., s.v. "Propitiation" by James Oliver Buswell, Jr.

[4]From the author's class notes, 1962.

[5]Barclay, *Crucified and Crowned*, p. 100.

[6]Billy Graham, *Peace With God* (New York: Doubleday, 1953), pp. 98-99.

CHAPTER 5

Justification

The term *justification* comes from the world of forensics, the discipline concerned with the rationale used to support a position in debate. Our courts of law deal in forensics. For example, *justification* takes place when an attorney demonstrates to the court that his client cannot legitimately be declared guilty. The defendant's actions are shown to be just; therefore, all charges against him must be dropped.

I know of a situation in which all the local anesthesiologists banded together and refused to work with a particular neurosurgeon they judged to be medically incompetent. Even though the surgeon in question admitted on the witness stand that he had operated on the wrong side of a patient's brain on at least one occasion, he alleged that the anesthesiologists had no right to challenge his competency. The court ruled in favor of the anesthesiologists. Their victory is regarded as a landmark decision in trials of this nature. Now that the court's verdict has successfully cleared the appellate courts, the anesthesiologists can never be brought to trial again on the same charge. Forensically speaking, they have been justified.

The Bible uses the term *justification* in precisely the same sense. Grace isn't an arbitrary action. Our record has to be cleared so that we may stand before the divine tribunal with the assurance that no legitimate charge can be brought against us. Since we are, in fact, guilty as charged, another method of justification has to become operational. This is done through the Atonement.

The biblical doctrine of justification has been called "the apex of Christianity."[1] Martin Luther spoke of it as the "doctrine of the standing or falling of the church."[2] As Christians, we should be interested in justification because grace is impossible without it.

Our Need for Justification

We've already discussed the universality of sin. Paul's statement in Romans 3:23 extends the guilt of sin to every mentally competent person on the earth: "All have sinned and fall short of the glory of God." Our sin has alienated us from God. He is just and righteous, but we are guilty of having transgressed. When we are measured beside a holy God, we are all shown to be terribly inadequate.

Since "there is none righteous, no, not one" (Romans 3:10, KJV), we need someone else to deal with the sin problem so that we may somehow be treated as though we are just. We need more than mercy. In a forensic sense, mercy usually results in a reduced sentence. When a guilty felon pleads for mercy in our legal system, he is usually asking for a reduction in the penalty. If the offense requires a jail term, he throws himself on the mercy of the court, hoping for a suspended sentence or a fine. Mercy, in that sense, won't do us any good when God sits in judgment on the human race. What we need is pardon.

Pardon goes beyond mercy. The nature of pardon in our legal system is illustrated by the well-known presidential one extended to former President Nixon. On August 9, 1974, the president resigned his office rather than face the humiliation of almost certain impeachment. Even though his resignation spared the nation the trauma of an impeachment trial, the question of the president's guilt in covering up the Watergate affair remained an unresolved issue.

Leon Jaworski, the special prosecutor, remained on the job. Had Mr. Jaworski been able to produce evidence of criminal behavior, Mr. Nixon could have been forced to accept the humiliation of being declared a criminal and sentenced to some form of judicial punishment. That possibility was averted later in the same year when Gerald Ford, the new president, granted Mr. Nixon an executive pardon for any crimes he may have committed while in office. The wisdom of Mr. Ford's decision is still being debated, but the fact remains that Mr. Nixon received an executive pardon and therefore cannot be brought to trial.

Our pardon is provided through the death of Jesus. We don't have to settle for a reduced sentence. Thus, we can never again be charged for the wrongs that have corrupted our past lives: "For all have sinned and fall short of the glory of God, and are justified freely by his grace through the redemption that came by Christ Jesus" (Romans 3:23-24).

God's act of pardon takes away the stigma of guilt, the burden of separation from Him, and the dread of eternal condemnation. On the other hand, the only possible outcome for the unjustified sinner is "the forfeiture of eternal life and the ghastly thirst of the soul . . . irrevocable banishment from God's presence."[3]

Freely Given

Paul's use of the term *freely* must be appreciated if we are to understand God's grace correctly. He chose the Greek word *dorean*, which suggests that "our justification is bestowed on us as a gift; it is not earned by nor do we make requital for it."[4]

American culture has popularized the slogan, "There is no free lunch." Practically every benefit that comes to the human race is attained by some kind of human effort. One athletic team defeats another because the winning players train harder, play a more disciplined game, and persevere longer than the members of the opposing team. Of course, having bigger, stronger, and faster athletes has something to do with it, too.

According to free enterprise theory, wealth is the result of effort. The person who gets to work earlier, exceeds minimal job requirements, stays after hours, and comes in on Saturdays is probably going to be the one who gets promoted. The only other way to get promoted is to be the son of the man who owns the business. In either case, human cause is connected with reward.

Furthermore, when we compensate others, it's usually because we have a vested interest. During the fall, I have been seen sitting in the bleachers rooting for a certain high-school football team. Eight different high schools play football in our metropolitan area, but I always support the Washington Warriors. I don't support them because they always have the best athletes or because I like their coach. I don't cheer for them because their colors are red and blue. I root for Washington High School because my children have played in the band. My enthusiasm springs from my vested interest.

That mind-set makes it harder for us to understand how God rewards us without any human cause. We've done nothing to endear ourselves to Him. On the contrary, we've all rebelled: "We all, like sheep, have gone astray" (Isaiah 53:6). God was under no obligation to save us. His program of redemption flows from His love and not from any kind of debt that He owed.

In contrast to God's willingness to freely forgive us our sins without considering any merit on our part, consider the man who goes to the pay window at his place of employment on Friday afternoon. He doesn't feel he is receiving a gift from his employer when he picks up his check. He is receiving compensation in return for the use of his skills and his energy on the job. The kingdom of God doesn't function that way, however. It's true that we use our skills and contribute our time and energy to the cause of Christ, but the rewards we receive from God are not to be viewed as wages. Paul said about this issue, "Now when a man works, his wages are not credited to him as a gift, but as an obligation. However, to the man who does not work but trusts God who justifies the wicked, his faith is credited as righteousness" (Romans 4:4-6).

The biblical command to be baptized clouds this concept in the minds of some. Members of the evangelical community generally reject baptism as a conversion act because they have assumed that baptism would be a qualifying work if it were viewed as a prerequisite to salvation. On the other hand, one must do some fancy hermeneutical footwork to explain away the fact that the Bible connects baptism with salvation in several different places. In Acts 2:38, it's linked to the forgiveness of sins. According to Acts 22:16, sins are washed away when one is baptized. Romans 6:3-4 connects it with the Atonement. Galatians 3:26-27 presents it as an act of faith enabling us to become clothed with Christ. Baptism is directly related to salvation in 1 Peter 3:21. One must ignore a rather massive amount of biblical testimony to conclude that baptism is merely an "outward sign of an inward grace." The evidence forces us to conclude with G. R. Beasley-Murray that "the idea that baptism is a pure symbolic rite must be pronounced not alone unsatisfactory, but out of harmony with the New Testament itself."[5]

If we are to accept baptism as an act of conversion, however, we must harmonize that premise with the teaching that justification is freely given without any human qualification or merit. Some of the controversy surrounding baptism can be erased if we simply realize that baptism marks the *time* of our relationship change. It has nothing to do with the *reason* for our transformation. In terms of merit, we are indeed *saved by grace plus nothing*!

Paul described the grace program this way:

> But when the kindness and love of God our Savior appeared, he saved us, not because of righteous things we had done, but because of his mercy. He saved us through the washing of rebirth and renewal by the Holy Spirit, whom he poured out on us generously through Jesus Christ our Savior, so that, having been justified by his grace, we might become heirs having the hope of eternal life (Titus 3:4-7).

What causes God to respond so generously to our need? The only answer is that we are made in His image and created according to His likeness (Genesis 1:26-27). The picture we get from Genesis is that the human race represents the highest achievement in God's program of creation. He loves His creation too much to assign the entire human race to torment. Thus, He offers a program to rescue fallen humankind from the "broad road that leads to destruction." That's what grace is all about.

Grace—The Basis of Self-Esteem

Because we are justified freely by the grace of God, we have a legitimate claim to self-worth. Many people think self-esteem is achieved when they climb the success ladder. They assume that people automatically feel good about themselves when they achieve fame and fortune. If that's the case, how do we explain the tragic lives of people like Freddie Prinze, Janis Joplin, and Howard Hughes? These people and many others like them were vocationally successful for a time, but they left this life as despondent failures.

Unfortunately, Christians sometimes find themselves running down the same track. They become thing oriented, production centered, and achievement conscious. The church that can't flash ever-increasing numbers on the attendance board and show an upward spiraling trend in contributions is often looked upon as a dead church. Relationships and spiritual growth can be flourishing, yet the church may still be looked upon in negative terms because the dollars and the numbers aren't "right." It's amazing how we use the world's standards of success to measure the vitality of spiritual activities.

Our worth in the sight of God isn't determined by the size of the church budget. Our worth is determined by the fact that God places supreme value on the personhood of every individual member of the church. Paul saw himself as a valuable servant of the kingdom, but he never boasted about attendance figures and contribution increases. His sense of self-worth was based on his relationship with God: "The grace of our Lord was poured out on me abundantly, along with the faith and love that are in Christ Jesus" (1 Timothy 1:14). A person's worth isn't determined by how well he makes his mark in the world of commerce and industry, by the size of his bank account, nor even by his identification with successful church programs. His worth is determined by the way God regards him!

In our zeal to convict men and women of their sins, we sometimes make it sound as if our sinful nature renders us worthless beings in God's sight. One of our hymns asks, "Would he devote that sacred head for such a worm as I?" Even John Newton's classic hymn "Amazing Grace" contains the unfortunate phrase, "that saved a *wretch* like me."

God has a higher view of us than that. We are created "a little lower than the heavenly beings" (Psalm 8:5). Even the non-Christian slave owners are said to "be worthy of full respect" (1 Timothy 6:1). The inherent worth of mankind is indicated by Peter's admonition to "show proper respect to everyone" (1 Peter 2:17). Although some theological systems place heavy emphasis on inherited sin, Jesus views children as being sinless; He has indicated that adults must become like children in order to enter God's kingdom (Matthew 18:3).

We have worth because we've been made in God's image and because God has chosen to honor us by arranging for us to be redeemed from the life of sin that we have willingly chosen. That's really the gist of John

3:16. We reap the benefits of Christ's substitutionary atonement because "God so loved the world." Left to our own inclinations and appetites, we may well be described as wretches and worms. But God doesn't see us that way. He considers us to be objects of compassion.

> Compared with . . . secular perspectives, the Christian view of self esteem is in a category by itself. It alone elevates men above the animals. It alone provides a solid foundation for self esteem. The Biblical view of man acknowledges our sins and fallacies, but it doesn't demean our deepest significance as creations of the living God. . . . Because we are created in the image of God, we possess worth, significance and value. We are saved by God, and deserving of the love of ourselves and others.[6]

What Justification Means to the Contemporary World

Some people think the place to discuss justification is behind the ivy-colored walls of a theological seminary. To them, the subject has very little relevance to people whose interests lie elsewhere. The truth is that the biblical concept of justification touches the lives of all kinds of people in every type of culture and setting.

Justification is relevant to contemporary man because it brings him to the realization that when he becomes a Christian, he is no longer cut off from God. The pain, suffering, loneliness, and disappointment that people encounter in life can be quite devastating. The loss of health, the loss of jobs, the death of loved ones, alienation from family members, and even conflicts with other Christians sometimes pile up until people start feeling they are coping with unbearable pressures. Some people are so overwhelmed that they begin to think their situation is hopeless. And it doesn't help all that much just to tell them they need to forget their worries and start trusting God.

I'll never forget a young black man whom I shall call Jesse. Jesse was paralyzed from his waist down. In desperation, he reached out for Christ. He turned to the yellow pages and started looking for a church because he figured someone there could tell him about Jesus. He called the church where I happened to serve on the ministerial staff. Studies followed, and Jesse was baptized into Christ. But he entered a predominantly white congregation where the brethren really didn't go out of their way to build friendship ties. No one would have denied him a place in the kingdom, but then he wasn't exactly welcomed with open arms either. His black friends, who weren't Christians, taunted him because he had accepted "the white man's religion." His physical problems got worse. The last time I saw him, he was lying on a gurney in a hospital ward. He started talking with me about his troubles. At length, I said, "Jesse, you've got to keep trusting the Lord." He looked at me with a strange expression. It started out as a grin, and I thought it changed to something like a sneer. Then he said, "It sure is easy to say, isn't it?"

I'm afraid I didn't help Jesse that much, but even so, a discouraged person needs to know that God is on his side. Even when life deals you a miserable set of cards, you have the assurance of knowing that your tie with God remains intact. That was Paul's perspective when he said, "I consider that our present sufferings are not worth comparing with the glory that will be revealed in us" (Romans 8:18).

The relevance of justification is also demonstrated by the fact that our acceptance in God's eyes enables us to be conscious of our purpose for living. Too many people are floating like driftwood on a swollen river. We're confronted with an overwhelming number of people in the world who could best be described by the anonymous author of the following verse:

> Into the world to eat and to sleep
>   And to know no reason why he was born
> Save to consume the corn
>   Devour the cattle, flock and fish
> And leave behind an empty dish.

Justification changes all that. We are rescued from emptiness and offered exciting challenges. From the perspective of justification, we can see every day of our lives bursting with opportunity to serve God. A cynic of our time has written, "Man comes here against his will and goes away disappointed." Persons who are justified by grace know that he completely missed the mark. They acknowledge and trust in these words: "And those he predestined, he also called; those he called, he also justified; those he justified, he also glorified" (Romans 8:30).

Summary and Conclusion

Justification is a forensic term used in a court of law to exonerate an accused person of charges that have been brought against him. The atoning blood of Christ is the justifying factor that spiritually clears our record in the divine tribunal of justice. Our need for the intervention of Christ in this process is rooted in our inability to defend ourselves. We stand self-condemned. Our lives confirm the validity of the charge that we have all sinned and fallen short of the glory of God.

Since God is holy, we must be "made righteous" in His sight before He can justify us. Through the Atonement, we are declared to be righteous, and we are allowed to wear the garments of righteousness—even though we are not and never can be actually righteous through our own efforts.

This righteousness is not grounded in any human behavior. There is no way to qualify for God's favor. Obedience flows from our lives in response to God's favor. It's not to be seen as a means of earning God's approval. Although baptism is indeed essential to salvation, it must be seen as the *time* a person receives forgiveness and not as the *reason* for his salvation.

Our awareness of our justification on the basis of Christ's work on Calvary increases our self-esteem as we come to realize the magnitude of God's love. If God thought we were valuable enough to allow His Son to die for us, we must have great worth indeed.

Thought Questions

1. What is meant by the word *forensic?*
2. How is the term *justified* applied in a legal sense?
3. How does Gerald Ford's pardon of former President Nixon illustrate the justification principle?

4. Is there a difference between mercy and pardon?
5. What are the implications of this statement: "We point to baptism as an answer to the question of *when* we are saved and not *why*"?
6. What is the meaning of the expression "freely given"?
7. Why did God respond to the human race so generously?
8. Consider how self-esteem among Christians differs from worldly self-esteem philosophy.
9. Suggest some implications of these phrases: "such a worm as I" and "saved a wretch like me."
10. How does the subject of justification affect our lives?

Notes

[1]*Zondervan Pictorial Encyclopedia of the Bible*, 3d printing, s.v. "Justification" by L. M. Peterson. 1975.

[2]Ibid.

[3]John R. W. Stott, *Basic Christianity* (London: Intervarsity Fellowship, 1958; Grand Rapids, Mich.: Eerdmans, 1966), p. 74.

[4]Moses E. Lard, *Commentary on the Letter to the Romans* (Lexington, Ky.: 1875; Des Moines, Iowa: Gospel Broadcast, n.d.), p. 116.

[5]G. R. Beasley-Murray, *Baptism in the New Testament* (Exeter, Devon, U.K.: 1962; Grand Rapids, Mich.: Eerdmans, 1986), p. 263.

[6]S. Bruce Narramore in *You Are Somebody Special*, cited by Gary Collins, *Christian Counseling* (Waco, Tex.: Word, 1980), p. 348.

C H A P T E R 6

Law and Grace

An adult Bible class was discussing grace one Sunday morning when the leader asked several members to contribute ideas about the way grace works. One person said, "When we try as hard as we can to obey all the commands of God, we still fall short. Grace takes up the slack and makes it possible for God to forgive us." Another suggested, "We work as if everything depends on us, and then we pray as if everything depends on God."

In my attempts to share the gospel, I used to tell people that grace is God's part in salvation and that obedience is man's part. I usually followed that up with a string of Bible references dealing with man's part and a verse or two about God's part. One day, I was sharing "man's part" with a woman who was interested in knowing God's will for her life. After I had outlined all the requirements under the heading of "man's part," she asked, "But what if I can't do all that?"

On another occasion, I went to the hospital to pray with a brother who was about to undergo surgery. He had stopped attending services because he didn't think he was "good enough to call himself a Christian." He was quite apprehensive about the possible outcome of the surgery. We talked about his relationship with God, and I tried to convince him that he was being too hard on himself. I said, "God only expects you to do the best you can." He responded by saying, "That's just the problem. I can't figure out what my best is." The man was uneducated, but I came away feeling he'd just shot a big hole in my "seat of the pants" theology.

These anecdotes are typical of many conversations about grace. In the American Restoration Movement, our long suit has been an emphasis on obedience. We're vaguely aware of the fact that grace is somehow connected with salvation, but we're a little afraid to put too much confidence in it. After all, if you preach too much grace, folks may get careless about doing what the Bible says.

Grace may well be more attractive to us if we understand that grace serves one set of needs and law serves an entirely different set. Our goal in this chapter is to sort out the different functions of these two important principles.

The Concept of Covenant

We claim the blessing of salvation because God has made a covenant with the human race. Jeremiah 31:31 introduces the prospect of God's arranging to introduce an entirely new covenant with the house of Israel and the house of Judah. Under the new covenant, people are promised that sins will be erased from the divine memory: "For I will forgive their wickedness and will remember their sins no more" (Jeremiah 31:34).

The term *covenant* isn't used much in modern conversation, but we need to develop a working definition of it in order to appreciate what God has done for us. *Covenant,* in ancient literature, primarily signified a disposition of property by will or otherwise. . . . In contradistinction to the English word (lit., a coming together), which signifies a mutual undertaking between two parties or more, each binding himself to fulfill obligations. It does not in itself contain the idea of joint obligation. It mostly signifies an obligation undertaken by a single person.[1]

The biblical usage of *covenant* suggests the following characteristics:

1. *It is a joint agreement between two parties.*

2. *It is usually initiated by one party.* In Jeremiah 31, the new covenant is initiated by God. The agreement isn't subject to any kind of bargaining process.

3. *It is often ratified by a sign.* God ratified His promise to exempt the world from future destruction by flood when He set the rainbow in the sky (Genesis 9:12-15). That was God's way of saying, "You can count on Me to stand behind My promise."

4. *It offers positive benefits to the person who receives it.* In Jeremiah 31, "forgiveness of sins" is the proclaimed benefit. We have no motive for entering into a covenant if no compensation is offered. The new covenant takes on meaning in our lives because it offers release from the oppressive burden of guilt.

5. *It obligates the one who receives the benefits.* A covenant by its very nature requires some form of response from the one to whom it is being offered. A summation of the old covenant requirements is reported in Micah 6:8: "And what does the LORD require of you? To act justly and to love mercy and to walk humbly with your God." The new covenant doesn't repeal those requirements. Grace in no way nullifies responsibility.

The New Covenant

The Jeremiah passage anticipates the new covenant. The word *new* suggests that an old covenant at some point in history governed God's people. It also implies that God looked toward a time when the older covenant would become obsolete. The Hebrew writer insists that under Christ, the prophecy of Jeremiah 31 has been fulfilled: "By calling this covenant 'new,' he has made the first one obsolete; and what is obsolete and aging will soon disappear" (Hebrews 8:13).

Sometimes we display little awareness of the reason for the change in covenants. Some Christians think of it as a flawed legal system being replaced by a perfect legal system. However, we must recognize that the problem with the old covenant wasn't with its law. Paul praised the law: "We know that the law is spiritual" (Romans 7:14). In Galatians 3:21, he wrote, "Is the law, therefore, opposed to the promises of God? Absolutely not! For if a law had been given that could impart life, then righteousness would certainly have come by the law." Those statements clearly rule out a streamlined law system as a basis for justification.

Why, then, was a new covenant necessary? Scripture provides a number of insights. First, *the law was not based on faith:* "The law is not based on faith; on the contrary, 'The man who does these things will live by them' " (Galatians 3:12). We shouldn't understand the apostle to imply that faith was lacking in all the people who lived under the old covenant. Paul was viewing law as a justifying principle; he wasn't thinking of its regulatory provisions. In verse 11, the apostle wrote, "Clearly no one is justified before God by the law, because, 'The righteous will live by faith.' " In the Greek, there is no article before the term for *law*. Literally, Paul might be understood to have said, "No one is justified before God by law."

In this sense, *salvation is by grace plus nothing!* As justifying principles, grace and law are mutually exclusive concepts. If one principle can indeed bring justification, the other one is necessarily eliminated. Scripture clearly establishes the distinction. In Romans 6:15, Paul flatly stated, "We are not under law but under grace." In Romans 11, he argued that Israel's saved remnant had been chosen by grace: "And if by grace, then it is no longer by works; if it were, grace would no longer be grace" (Romans 11:6). Neither statement was designed to encourage Christians to adopt an antinomian (against law) posture. If you look at the context of Romans 6, you can't miss the fact that the whole chapter is an appeal to Christians to live disciplined lives. Paul brought in grace so his readers would understand the nature of the justifying principle. It's all grace. We can't be saved partially by law keeping and partially by grace.

Second, *the sacrificial system of the law couldn't effectively deal with sin.* The writer of Hebrews made the point that it was impossible for the blood of bulls and goats to take away sin (Hebrews 10:4). That doesn't mean that the people who lived under the old covenant were unforgiven. The New Testament claims that the blood Jesus shed on the cross flowed both ways (Hebrews 9:15). In Jewish terminology, He is presented as the high priest who "by one sacrifice . . . has made perfect forever those who are being made holy" (Hebrews 10:14). It's pointless to debate whether the sins of the Israelites were rolled forward or if the blood of Christ flowed backward. God doesn't live in the context of time. His plan for developing the new covenant took place in the context of eternity, not time, according to Ephesians 3:11.

Those who were saved in the Old Testament era were justified by grace. God's redemptive program is the same for all people. The law system was never designed as a program of justification. "Paul did not, as some people interpret him, argue that justification and the Mosaic covenant depended on keeping the law—Romans 4:16– 9:22. One under the law was justified by faith, not by law. Justification by law was a Pharisaic distortion."[2]

Third, *the new covenant is aimed at the human heart.* The Hebrew writer related the prophecy of Jeremiah in the following words:

> This is the covenant I will make with the house of Israel
>> after that time, declares the Lord.
> I will put my laws in their minds
>> and write them on their hearts.
> I will be their God,
>> and they will be my people (Hebrews 8:10).

The writer's use of the Jeremiah passage implies that the old covenant was defective in the way it was transferred to human hearts. F. F. Bruce's comment on the Hebrew writer's usage of the term *law* is worth considering: "The original wording of Jeremiah 31:33 is, 'I will put my *torah* within them.' Heb. *torah* means more than statutory law; it embraces the idea of guidance and instruction."[3]

When the Jeremiah passage is compared to the statement of Ezekiel 11:19, the inadequacy of the law is clarified: "I will give them an undivided heart and put a new spirit in them; I will remove from them their heart of stone and give them a heart of flesh." In the redemptive work of Christ, we receive a new nature. Paul spoke of this new inward nature when he wrote, "I no longer live, but Christ lives in me" (Galatians 2:20). The new covenant renders the old covenant obsolete because it has the power through grace to transform human nature.

The Purpose of the Law

Although the law of Moses proved to be a totally ineffective system of justification, it did have many beneficial purposes. Reviewing some of them will deepen our appreciation for the law.

1. *It had a civil purpose.* Robert Milligan observes,

> The law was given to the Jews for the purposes of civil government. In this respect it was well adapted to the development, and happiness of the individual and the family as well as the tribe and the nation.[4]

Israel was a theocracy. Thus it's not surprising to find tax laws, criminal codes and property regulations within the Pentateuch.

2. *It had a regulatory purpose.* Paul wrote, "We know that the law is good if a man uses it properly. We also know that the law is not made for good men, but for lawbreakers" (1 Timothy 1:8-9). Law keeps people in line. If a man doesn't have some kind of law, then all restrictions are removed and anarchy prevails. The law of Moses served that purpose. We are still "under law to Christ" according to 1 Corinthians 9:21. Grace doesn't take away the need for obedient living. Paul wrote, "Shall we go on sinning that grace may increase? By no means. We died to sin. How can we live any longer therein?" (Romans 6:1-2).

3. *It had an educational purpose.* Law increases the awareness of sin. Paul said, "I would not have known that it's a sin to covet if the law had not said, 'Thou shalt not covet.'" (Romans 7:7). The Jew had an advantage on the Gentile because he had been "entrusted with the Word of God." Because of the law, the Jews developed an understanding of God's desires for the human race that could never have been comprehended by the pagan mind. Look at the first four commands which were handed to Moses on Mount Sinai. Not one of the four could have been figured out by an untaught pagan, no matter how sharp and how morally sensitive he might have been. The law educated the Jews in these areas.

The law served yet another educational purpose for Israel, in that it stood as a sort of shadow—a promising yet indistinct barometer of the future. Paul spoke of the Sabbath and the Jewish feast days as a "shadow of the things that were to come" (Galatians 2:16).

When I was a young boy, Shredded Wheat came in a package that featured a picture of Niagara Falls on the front. I often looked at that two-dimensional image and tried to visualize what it would be like to witness this great natural wonder with my own eyes. Many years later, I moved to upstate New York and had many occasions to visit the Falls. My concept was no longer limited to what I saw printed on cardboard. I saw the real thing. I heard the roar of the water as it cascaded over the American Falls. I felt the spray of the mist from the water as it splashed against my face. I was close enough to almost touch the rampaging Niagara River. I saw the mountains of ice that form in the river during winter. I did just about everything except ride a barrel over the

Horseshoe Falls. My contact with the Falls when I saw it on the cereal box was mostly imagination; my contact with the Falls in Ontario and New York was real. The law served as a kind of cereal box picture of God's redemptive program; Jesus presents it to us in reality.

4. *It had a redemptive purpose.* According to Galatians 3:24, "the law was put in charge to lead us to Christ." The King James Version uses the word *schoolmaster* to describe the purpose of the law. That's a little misleading because most of us think about a teacher when we hear that word. We miss Paul's main point if we perceive the schoolmaster as a teacher.

> "Schoolmaster" is a tr. of παιδγωγός, *Paidogogos*, lit. "child leader." This *paidogogos* was not a teacher but a slave in wealthy families to whom the general oversight of a boy was committed. It was his duty to accompany his charge to and from school, never to lose sight of him in public, to prevent association from objectionable companions, to inculcate moral lessons at every opportunity. . . . Naturally, to the average boy, the *paidogogos* must have represented the incorporation of everything resented. Hence St. Paul's figure must be paraphrased, "the law was *paidagogos*, necessary but irksome to direct us until the time of Christ."[5]

As the law increases human awareness of sin, desperation takes over, and men begin to realize they can't lift themselves up by their own bootstraps. Law makes us aware of sin, and in that sense, it's beneficial. But just as the *paidagogos* became burdensome to a Jewish boy, so law can become a burden to us. The more law we know, the more guilty we feel. This appears to be Paul's point in Romans 7. He became so familiar with law and so sensitive to his wrongdoing that he found himself tangled in a set of circumstances where he was doing the very thing he didn't want to do. Toward the end of the chapter, he expressed his complete frustration: "What a wretched man I am! Who will rescue me from this body of death?" (Romans 7:24).

In a sense, the law as a *paidogogos* helps with our redemption because it sensitizes us to the presence of sin in our lives, and that sets the stage for us to realize our need for a Savior. Paul's sense of wretchedness could not be alleviated until he came to grips with the saving work of Jesus. That was when he joyously proclaimed, "Therefore, there is now no condemnation for those who are in Christ Jesus, because through Christ Jesus the law of the Spirit of life set me free from the law of sin and death" (Romans 8:1-2).

Summary and Conclusion

Although many people like to think that our salvation takes place partly as the result of grace and partly as the result of law keeping, grace and law are actually two mutually exclusive principles of being made just. Salvation cannot be extended as just payment for correct law keeping and as a matter of grace at the same time.

Although the salvation of sinners is bestowed by grace under both covenants, the picture becomes clearer when the new covenant is seen in comparison with the old covenant. The term *covenant* refers to an agreement between God and man. God determines the benefits and establishes the conditions under which the blessings of the covenant are to be enjoyed.

God initiated a change because the law was not based on faith. The new covenant is received in consideration of a trusting, obedient faith. Furthermore, the sacrificial system under the old covenant was totally inadequate as a means of atoning for human sin. The old covenant was intended to touch the hearts of people, but most who adhered to it got bogged down in legalistic tradition. The new covenant caters to heart obedience.

Although we cannot be saved by keeping law, law does serve beneficial purposes. We are even under law to Christ. The law served a civil purpose for Israel. It helped Israel regulate behavior, and it continues to do the very same thing today. Law serves an educational purpose as it fine-tunes our perception of right and wrong, and it serves a redemptive purpose in the preparatory sense as it makes individuals aware of the need for a Savior.

> Not the labor of my hands
> Can fulfill the law's demands.
> Could my zeal no respite know,
> Could my tears forever flow
> All for sin could not atone,
> Thou must save and thou alone.
>   —"Rock of Ages"
>   by A. M. Toplady

Thought Questions

1. Why is it impossible for salvation to be partially by grace and partially by law?
2. What is the meaning of the term *covenant?*
3. In what way is the covenant new?

4. Why did Paul say, "The law was not based on faith"?
5. In what sense is salvation by grace plus nothing?
6. Does the Old Testament actually teach justification by law? Or is that a Pharisaic distortion?
7. What is meant by, "I will put my laws in their minds and write them on their hearts"?
8. What were the purposes of the law of Moses?
9. What are the purposes of being "under law to Christ?"
10. How does the term *schoolmaster*, as used in Galatians 3:24 of the King James Version, mislead us?

Notes

[1]W. E. Vine, *Expository Dictionary of New Testament Words* (Old Tappan, N. J.: Fleming H. Revell, 1966), I: 250-51.

[2]Thomas Olbricht, "Covenant and Law in the New Testament," *Firm Foundation*, September 10, 1963, p. 583.

[3]F. F. Bruce, *The Epistle to the Hebrews—New International Commentary on the New Testament* (Grand Rapids, Mich.: Eerdmans, 1964), p. 172.

[4]Robert Milligan, *The Scheme of Redemption* (St. Louis: Bethany Press, 1960), p. 83.

[5]*International Standard Bible Encyclopedia*, 1955 ed., s.v. "Schoolmaster" by Burton Scott Easton.

CHAPTER 7

Faith and Works

Grace has become the subject of bitter controversy among people of faith. However much we might regret the controversy that surrounds the subject of faith and works, we must consider it because so much is at stake.

All persons who accept the Bible as the standard for defining our relationship with God accept the premise that we participate in God's blessings through the avenue of faith. But believers part company in their attempts to understand when faith becomes effective. This whole area of discussion generates several questions. Are we saved by faith alone? If so, what is meant by "faith alone"? Are we saved by a combination of faith and works? Are there different kinds of faith? Where does obedience fit into God's program? Is baptism connected with salvation in any way?

Paul on Faith

Many students of the Bible regard Paul's statement in Ephesians 2:8-10 as a representative expression of his teaching concerning faith and works:

> For it is by grace you have been saved, through faith—and this not from yourselves, it is the gift of God—not by works, so that no one can boast.

For we are God's workmanship, created in Christ
Jesus to do good works, which God prepared in
advance for us to do.

The letter to the Ephesians is addressed to "the saints
in Ephesus" (1:1). The primary readers were already
Christians. Paul had spent a portion of three years living
and working among those people. Acts 19 presents a
picture of Christians living in a hostile, pagan environment. Prostitutes practiced their profession as an act of
worship within the walls of the temple of Artemis, one
of the seven wonders of the ancient world. Greed and
the profit motive dominated the mind-set of many Ephesian residents. They became threatened when the idol
sales dropped off as a result of Paul's evangelistic success,
and a large number of them rioted. They gathered in the
theater and chanted, "Great is Artemis of the Ephesians,"
until they were hoarse. The wild spectacle continued
until the town clerk was finally able to restore a semblance
of order.

It's safe to assume that Christians felt a certain amount
of stress. They were squeezed on the one side by the
emotional frenzy of the pagan community and on the
other by the demands of an enlightened conscience. Paul
wrote to help them make a clean mental break with the
old life and its value system. He used sinister language
to describe their former circumstances: "As for you, you
were dead in your transgressions and sins, in which you
used to live when you followed the ways of this world
and the ruler of the kingdom of the air, the spirit who
is now at work in those who are disobedient" (Ephesians
2:1-2).

The apostle made no attempt to gloss over the degener-
ate past. He wanted his readers to understand "that at
that time you were separate from Christ, excluded from
citizenship in Israel and foreigners to the covenants of
the promise, without hope and without God in the world"
(Ephesians 2:12).

The Ephesian letter was written to encourage those
disciples in their struggle against the hostility of their
environment, and a part of the effort to uplift them
included an explanation of the grace program. Although
they had once been in the grasp of the "ruler of the
kingdom of the air," they had been released from their
spiritual enslavement through Christ. Paul stated, "But
because of his great love for us, God, who is rich in
mercy, made us alive with Christ even when we were
dead in transgressions—it is by grace you have been
saved" (Ephesians 2:4-5).

Verses 8-10 discuss how the grace program works. The
Ephesian Christians had received "the gift of God." The
controversy begins over that point. What is the gift?
Some theologians get so bogged down in linguistic arguments that they never come to appreciate the immensity
of the gift. It simplifies our understanding of the passage,
and eliminates the need for engaging in pointless debate,
if we think of the grace, faith, and salvation *package* as
the gift of God.

We really have no difficulty discerning that grace is a
gift from God, and we can readily comprehend that
salvation is a gift from God. Our problem stems from
understanding that *faith* is a part of the gifts package.
Faith is clearly a human response to God, so how can it
be considered a gift *from* God *to* us? It's a gift in the
sense that God has agreed to give us credit for righteous-

ness when we express faith toward Him. God gave us the capacity for faith, and He made it possible for faith to have a meaningful effect. In Romans 4:5, Paul commented, "To the man who does not work but trusts God who justifies the wicked, his faith is credited as righteousness." Paul's point in Ephesians seemed to be that everything that makes the salvation relationship possible is to be considered part of God's gift. Concerning the interrelationship between faith and grace, R. C. Bell notes, "Faith and grace are correlatives, implying each other, whereas merit and grace are antipodes, mutually exclusive. . . . Human merit and gospel grace are so contradictory everywhere that either disallows the other."[1]

Levels of Faith

To properly understand Paul's emphasis on faith, we must recognize that faith functions at three different levels.

The lowest level of faith is that of *acceptance;* one intellectually agrees that certain premises are true. All of us exhibit faith at this level, but sometimes that faith doesn't affect our lives very much at all. For example, most of us would accept the accuracy of the *Guinness Book of World Records.* Our belief in this instance is limited to mental agreement with the facts claimed in that volume; it doesn't affect the way we live.

It's possible to believe in God on the same level, to accept all the New Testament teachings concerning the nature of Christ without making any kind of life response. This very thing happened during the lifetime of Jesus. John said that "many even among the leaders believed in Him. But because of the Pharisees they would not confess their faith for fear they would be put out of the synagogue" (John 12:42). Paul didn't have this level of faith in mind when he concluded that we are justified by faith (Romans 5:1).

Faith also exists at the *trust* level. During a political campaign, candidates for office usually make promises to the voters. Over the years, the voters have learned that political promises are nothing more than election-year rhetoric. The astute voter is more interested in the integrity of the candidate than the programs he offers. In the final analysis, a voter marks his ballot in favor of a certain candidate because he believes in that office seeker. That's why elective office is often labeled a public trust.

Christian faith must also be exercised at the trust level if the grace of God is to become effective. The psalmist wrote, "Blessed is the man who makes the LORD his trust" (Psalm 40:4). Jesus worked diligently during His earthly ministry to build the trust level of faith in His disciples. After He rebuked the storm on the Sea of Galilee, He expressed His disappointment to the disciples: "Why are you so afraid? Do you still have no faith?" (Mark 4:40). He wasn't questioning their acceptance of intellectual propositions regarding His identity; He was saddened because they didn't trust Him. Paul appealed to the trust level of faith as he presented the rhetorical question, "If God is for us, who can be against us?" (Romans 8:31).

Faith must also express itself in *obedience*. Paul mentioned "the obedience that comes from faith" (Romans 1:5), and he claimed that the revelation of the mystery is "made known to all nations for the obedience of faith" (Romans 16:26, KJV).

According to popular evangelical theory, the requirement of obedience negates the faith principle. The media
evangelists assure their audiences that salvation occurs
when one is willing to "accept Christ as your personal
Savior." To demand more, in their view, makes salvation
a matter of works. They are correct in concluding that
the grace principle eliminates works as the basis of
salvation (see Romans 11:6). Strangely enough, practically every person who advocates "accepting Christ" as
the only condition of salvation has also been persuaded
to believe that character, habits, and lifestyles must be
altered before one can establish fellowship with God.
No evangelical minister, with any degree of integrity,
would eliminate repentance from God's program of redemption.

Repentance is obedience. Repentance demands action.
Billy Graham, perhaps the best known of all the evangelical spokespersons, does not hesitate to connect repentance
with action.

> Repentance is *first* and absolutely necessary if we
> are to be born again. It involves simple recognition
> of what we are before God—sinners who fell short
> of his glory; *second*, it involves genuine sorrow for
> sin; *third*, it means our willingness to turn from sin.[2]

Perhaps the evangelical community doesn't even realize
that it has accepted obedience as a part of the grace-faith
system. The demand for repentance negates the claim
that there is nothing for man to do in coming to Christ.
For most evangelicals, the aversion to obedience shows
up primarily in their rejection of baptism as an act of
conversion. Many evangelicals are sincerely convinced

that if baptism is included in the conversion process, it takes away from the grace concept.

The misunderstanding lies in a failure to comprehend the fact that baptism is an act of faith. J. D. Thomas has observed, "The expression of one's faith in obedience to commands, does not change the saving principle into non-faith."[3] The New Testament doesn't present baptism as a sacrament holding some kind of ritualistic cleansing power. When a person is baptized scripturally, that person is demonstrating his faith.

All those who accept an authoritative Bible agree that grace is appropriated through our faith. The writer of Hebrews stated, "And without faith it is impossible to please God, because anyone who comes to him must believe that he exists and that he rewards those who earnestly seek him" (Hebrews 11:6). Baptism lies within the perimeter of faith, and the Scriptures clearly include this act of faith in the salvation process. In Acts 22:16, Paul was told, "And now what are you waiting for? Get up, be baptized and wash your sins away, calling on [the name of the Lord]." A direct connection between faith and baptism was made in Galatians 3:26-27: "You are all sons of God through faith in Christ Jesus, for all of you who were baptized into Christ have clothed yourselves with Christ." Significantly, this statement came at the conclusion of a section in Paul's letter to the Galatians in which he had just established the premise that mere law cannot generate spiritual life.

In Ephesians 2:10, Paul referred to "good works" as the acts of service flowing from the newly begun relationship with God. Christian service is a reaction to God's gift. Some consider the life of service to be an attempt to qualify for heaven. In their view, the more works of

Christian charity one performs, the more points one accumulates in God's bookkeeping system. This is precisely why most churches have a rather sizable gathering of worshipers on Sunday morning, a much smaller crowd on Sunday night, and an even smaller Wednesday night assembly. Those who see attendance at the assembly as a means of qualifying for heaven find it convenient to rationalize themselves into meeting the minimal requirements. A person who thinks this way is usually pretty certain that observing the Lord's Supper is a minimal requirement. Consequently, he will show up at least once on the Lord's Day to make sure he communes. Some even go so far as to leave the assembly after the fruit of the vine has been served, thus avoiding the necessity of remaining for the collection and the sermon! To a person whose mind works this way, the Sunday night and Wednesday night assemblies are optional. The attendance records of most congregations will reveal the sad truth that many church members think this way.

In a vain effort to reverse this trend, church leaders have tried to convince members that the Sunday evening and Wednesday night assemblies are also essential. A story made the rounds a few years ago concerning two men standing in line awaiting judgment. Every few minutes, they would hear someone at the front of the line burst forth in ecstatic expressions of joy and everyone in earshot would applaud. Finally, one of the men who stood near the rear of the line decided he would go up to the front and see what was causing such a response. In a little while he came back and reported to his friend. He was grinning from ear to ear as he said, "Hooray! They're not counting Wednesday night."

The only difference between those people who think they can qualify for heaven by showing up when the communion is served and those who believe that one must get to the midweek service in order to qualify for heaven is the conviction about what constitutes an "essential" assembly. At the risk of emptying church houses, I'd like to suggest that we abandon all our arguments concerning "essential" assemblies. We need to spend a like amount of energy helping Christians understand the magnitude of God's gift. There is a place for giving instruction concerning the avenues through which a loving heart responds to God, and we should even point out that regular attendance at the assembly is one of these avenues. But the *primary* motive for attendance is the realization that we are "created in Christ Jesus to do good works."

Loving attitudes, unselfish service, and moral purity should never be viewed as attempts to prove ourselves worthy of being admitted into the gates of heaven. Our reasons for obeying God are best summed up in the following statement:

> First, it expresses faith in the manner designated by Scripture to allow the sinner to become a full heir in Christ. Second, it expresses the love of a Christian to Christ for the salvation he has been given and for the relationship with God in which he lives. Third, it expresses his trust in God and Christ and Their promises.[4]

James on Faith

In the sixteenth century, indulgence salesmen traveled throughout Europe hawking religious relics. They promised their customers a divine reprieve from the pain of purgatory. One of the most effective of these salesmen was John Tetzel, who worked the territory around Martin Luther's hometown in northern Germany. Tetzel would show up in town and emerge from an ornate carriage in his long, flowing clerical robes. He would display a small red cross. Then he would begin his pitch, which went something like this:

> This cross I now hold before you has all the forgiving power of the cross on which Jesus died. Think about your sins. This cross even has the power to secure pardon for sins which you will commit in the future. Think about it, my friends. You can receive letters which are properly certified to assure you of the deliverance of your father, your mother and all those dear departed loved ones who now writhe in the pain of purgatory. All that stands between them and deliverance from their agony is alms—a few trifling alms. Oh, if you could only hear your good mother as she pleads with you, "Have pity, oh my child!" Will you let your own mother, your departed brother, your child agonize in their tormenting flames. Remember my friends, "As soon as the coin in the coffer rings, the soul from purgatory springs."[5]

That was the environment in which Martin Luther lived when he nailed his ninety-five theses to the door of the Wittenberg church building on October 31, 1517.

As Luther reacted to the excesses of indulgence marketing, he came to the conclusion that salvation can never be accomplished by the work of man. He contended that human beings are justified by faith alone.[6] Since the Epistle of James seemed to be at odds with that conclusion, Luther's solution to the dilemma was to cast doubt on the canonicity of James. In 1522, he declared it to be an "epistle of straw."[7]

There has to be a better way of reconciling the views of James and Paul. Arbitrary rejection of the canonicity of James may resolve the conflict, but it's a little bit like the gardener who destroys his entire vegetable crop to get rid of one rabbit.

As a student of the Word approaches the controversial material in James 2, he needs to remember a few things about the context of the letter. First, James was writing to Jewish Christians. Second, he was writing a treatise on Christian ethics. Third, the faith-works passage came on the heels of a discussion about class discrimination in the church (2:1-10). And fourth, James was making practical application of the faith principle; he was not providing an exhaustive explanation of justification by faith.

Four points made in the faith-works section need to be understood by the reader of James.

1. *If faith is never expressed in concrete action, it doesn't really help anyone* (2:16-20). The writer illustrated his point by observing that compassionate thoughts toward the poor must be translated into compassionate deeds. Christians can't afford the luxury of sitting in comfortable church buildings and praying for the poor while people stand on their doorsteps naked and starving.

2. *Faith without action is useless* (2:20, 26). When I was a boy, we owned a family milk cow. She was our only source of milk. When she was dry, we went without. One year, our cow gave birth to a calf, which should have meant that we could expect to be enjoying her milk within a few days. Unfortunately, the cow died two or three days after the calf was born. To us, the greatest

loss (aside from our emotional attachment to "Elsie")
was the realization that we wouldn't be drinking milk.
Dead cows don't give milk. In like manner, dead faith,
no matter how promising it may look in prospect, cannot
produce any healthy spiritual benefits.

3. *Faith without works can be found in hell* (2:19). The
demons believe God exists. It scares them, but they never
express faith in either trust or obedience.

4. *Faith comes alive when it is expressed in good deeds*
(2:20-25). The author cited the examples of Abraham's
offering of his son, Isaac, and of Rahab's willingness to
protect the Hebrew spies from detection by their Ca-
naanite enemies. Thus, he wanted his readers to understand that "a person is justified by what he does and not
by faith alone" (2:24).

Can Paul and James Be Harmonized?

Martin Luther once offered his doctor's beret to anyone
who could successfully harmonize James and Paul.[8] Without wishing to claim Luther's beret, I propose the following suggestions as a set of guidelines for studying the two
different viewpoints on faith.

1. *James and Paul wrote for different audiences.* James
wrote to "the twelve tribes scattered among the nations"
(James 1:1). Paul's writings in Ephesians were aimed at
those who were "excluded from citizenship in Israel and
foreigners to the covenants of the promise" (Ephesians
2:12). In Ephesians, Paul was concerned about undergird-
ing the faith of the Gentile Christians; he did this by
deepening their appreciation for the salvation experience.
James, on the other hand, was concerned with Christian
behavior in the social setting.

2. *Paul and James wrote to correct different misconceptions.* Paul took aim at pride. He wanted the Ephesians to know that there was no ground for boasting because their salvation was a gift from God. James wrote to people who would take their salvation for granted. His audience consisted of those who thought they didn't have to do anything because they had faith. He wanted them to know that faith had to be expressed in action.

3. *Paul and James wrote about different levels of faith.* When James pointed out the inadequacy of faith alone, he was thinking of *historical* faith—the belief in the premise that God exists and that He has acted through Christ. James saw historical faith as being nonproductive if it remained on that level.

Paul had a totally different level of faith in view, which might be illustrated by the patient who visits his doctor complaining of a stuffy nose and a sore throat. The doctor says, "You've got a sinus infection and postnasal drainage. Here's a prescription for antibiotics. Take them for a week and the medicine should clear up your nose and throat." The patient's faith in his doctor begins with an acceptance of the diagnosis. He must also accept the claim that antibiotics will improve his health. The patient shows that he trusts his doctor by getting the prescription filled and by completing the recommended regimen. Paul's concept of faith included all three elements— acceptance, trust, and obedience.

4. *Paul and James supported each other's concept of faith.* James advocated a trusting faith: "If any one of you lacks wisdom, he should ask God, who gives generously to all without finding fault, and it will be given to him. But when he asks, he must believe and not doubt, because he who doubts is like a wave of the sea, blown and tossed

by the wind" (James 1:5-6). Paul even supported James
in the Ephesians passage. He saw good works flowing from
the faith life (Ephesians 2:10).

Summary and Conclusion

Sadly, the grand subject of faith and its relationship
to grace has been allowed to become the focal point of
bitter religious controversy. Much of the controversy
stems from a tendency to isolate certain segments of
Scripture and to build an entire theology around fragmen-
tary New Testament teaching.

Some see the approach of Paul as ruling out the
necessity of obedience. There just doesn't seem to be any
place for required obedience in a program of grace,
according to modern evangelical thought. However, even
that is taken with a degree of reservation because repentance and good moral behavior are seen as salvation
requirements. Others see James as an advocate of a
"do-it-yourself" salvation project, without giving much
credence to grace and faith as justifying principles.

It's impossible to comprehend the biblical message on
faith without recognizing the premise that faith is expressed on three different levels—acceptance, trust, and
obedience. Both Paul and James emphasized the obedience level, but they saw it from different perspectives,
much in the same way that coaches and referees see
athletic contests from different perspectives.

At the core of this entire matter must be an understanding that obedience is to be viewed as an act of faith,
never as a qualifying principle: "For the Christian, obedience is always an expression of love and faith. It is never

an attempt to earn salvation or to make oneself righteous through human achievement."[9]

Thought Questions

1. Why did Paul write to the Ephesians?
2. Why did Paul give an explanation of the grace-faith program to the Ephesians?
3. What is "the gift" of Ephesians 2:8?
4. Why is the acceptance level of faith insufficient as a justifying principle?
5. How would you answer the claim that the obedience requirement cancels the grace-faith program?
6. How does obedience fit into the grace-faith program?
7. Are the good works of which James and Paul spoke qualifying works?
8. What do you think Luther meant when he wrote that we are justified by "faith alone"?
9. What objective was James trying to achieve in discussing faith and works?
10. How would you harmonize James and Paul?

Notes

[1]R. C. Bell, *Studies in Ephesians* (Austin, Tex.: Firm Foundation Publishing House, n.d.), p. 15.

[2]Billy Graham, *How to be Born Again* (New York: Warner Books, 1979), p. 191.

[3]J. D. Thomas, *The Biblical Doctrine of Grace* (Abilene, Tex.: Biblical Research Press, 1977), p. 46.

[4]David Chadwell, *Beware of the Leaven of the Pharisees* (Abilene, Tex.: Quality Publications, 1985), pp. 60-61.

[5]See Roland Bainton, *Here I Stand—A Life of Luther* (New York:

Mentor Books, 1950), pp. 60-61. The author provides a graphic
description of the tactics used by Tetzel.

⁶Luther is often misrepresented at this point. Although it's true
that he taught justification by faith alone, his concept of justification
by faith alone and the concept that is popular among many contemporary evangelicals are at variance with each other. In *The Small
Catechism*, he said of baptism, "It works forgiveness of sins, delivers
from death and the devil, and confers everlasting salvation on all
who believe as the Word and promise of God declares." Joseph
Stump, *An Explanation of Luther's Small Catechism* (Philadelphia:
United Lutheran Publishing House, 1907), p. 23.

⁷Bainton, *Here I Stand*, pp. 259-61.

⁸Ibid., p. 259.

⁹Chadwell, *Beware of the Leaven of the Pharisees*, p. 61.

Legalism, an Enemy of Grace

I had just stepped out into the foyer to greet the worshipers as they left the church building. Friendly greetings and favorable remarks about the sermon were the order of the day. Then came a brother who always seemed to feel the need to teach the preacher the way of truth a little more perfectly by adding some significant details he thought should have been included in the sermon. "Preacher," he said, "there's one passage that we must remember above all others." And before I had a chance to say anything, he was rattling off James 2:10 out of his repository of King James memory verses, "For whosoever shall keep the whole law, and yet offend in one point, he is guilty of all." I contributed some deep theological insight like, "Yeah" (nothing so profound as "Amen"). I really didn't want to get him started. He jammed his finger against my chest and said, "Now, remember, preacher, if we fall short on just one little point, we've disobeyed God entirely."

That conversation probably stands out in my mind more than any other when the subject of legalism comes up. Legalists have very little use for grace. The legalistic mind-set concentrates more on the human response to the gospel than on the good news that Christ came into our world and took upon Himself the burden of our sins. Nevertheless, those who like to regard themselves as grace oriented often display legalistic tendencies. Joseph C. Aldrich challenges our smugness when he says of biblically oriented people, "We are all legalists by nature."[1]

Legalism spawns endless problems in the Christian community. It encourages division, robs Christians of their sense of security, promotes sectarianism, and often gives birth to sinful pride. Legalists hurt the reputation of the church. There are many sincere and even loving legalists, but the fact remains that legalism is an enemy of grace.

Legalism Defined

Trying to define legalism is a little bit like trying to come up with a definition for *wind*. It's tough to find just the right combination of words. *Webster's New Collegiate Dictionary* defines *legalism* as "a strict, literal or excessive conformity to the law or to a religious or moral code."[2] That narrows the focus and prevents us from using the word as a catchall label for everything we don't like, but the definition lacks precision. At what point is conformity to law considered strict, literal, or excessive? Perhaps the idea can be better communicated by noting some of the characteristics of legalism rather than trying to establish a textbook definition.

What Legalism Is Not

1. *Legalism is not biblical obedience.* The gospel includes commands that God expects His people to obey. John wrote, "This is love for God: to obey his commands. And his commands are not burdensome" (1 John 5:3).

Thomas Olbricht helps us to divide the territory between biblical obedience and legalistic requirements: "Legalism can never be employed to designate faithful obedience to the commands of God, whether ethical or ritual. The use of the term, therefore, should only be employed when speaking of a distortion of a law or command."[3]

2. *Literalism is not necessarily legalism.* The Bible contains both literal and symbolic language. One can become entangled in an interpretive nightmare if he attempts to attach literal meanings to some of the symbolism in the apocalyptic sections of Scripture, but most of the Bible consists of historical, instructive, and doctrinal material. This kind of data is nearly always given in straightforward, literal language. Bible believers insist that such literal language must be taken at face value. Some leaders in the early church sought to attach allegorical meanings to the biblical text. Such attempts tend to reflect the biases of the interpreter and ignore the normal rules of language usage. The grammatical-historical method of interpretation requires us to view the Scripture as we would any other kind of straight-from-the-shoulder literature:

> It requires that the Bible be understood according to the original meaning of texts, discovered by historical, linguistic and lexicographical research. It prohibits the interpreter from changing the original message to accommodate present attitudes, viewpoints or philosophies.[4]

A grace orientation in no way suggests that the student has the right to be subjective and shoddy in his approach to scriptural exegesis. Precision and accuracy in trying to determine the meaning of the biblical text must still be the goal. Legalism is not to be equated with a quest for accuracy in biblical interpretation.

3. *Affirming that conditions must be met in the conversion process is not legalism.* A human response is required of those who wish to receive the forgiveness of sin. Sometimes the human response is presented as if the actions we perform somehow qualify us to receive God's blessings.

But when the human conditions are presented in that way, grace is thwarted, and legalism takes over. It is at this point that we must be very careful lest we cross the line between the obedience of faith and legalistic rule keeping.

> Be it understood that no faction of the restoration church today regards themselves as being legalists, and that all factions would openly declare they believe in the essentiality of God's grace. However many believe and strongly affirm that a New Testament Christian is righteous and justified before God because (1) he is a member of the restoration church and (2) he is doing approved works. It is the act of obeying the right teaching which makes a member of Christ's church righteous.[5]

New Testament obedience is a response to Christ's sacrifice. Paul spoke of it as "the obedience that comes from faith" (Romans 1:5). It is not an attempt to appear righteous on the basis of what one has done. God's free gift is given only to those who want it, and faith is the means of appropriating that gift (Ephesians 2:8-10; Romans 4:5). Repentance and baptism aren't works in the sense of being qualifying acts. They are acts of faith. K. C. Moser writes, "But what is the relation of conditions of salvation to the remission of sins? They have no relation except through the blood of Christ."[6]

Characteristics of Legalism

1. *Legalism reduces Christianity to rule keeping.* Legalistic attitudes were at the core of the church problems discussed in Acts 15: "Some men came down from Judea to Antioch and were teaching the brothers: 'Unless you are circumcised, . . . you cannot be saved' " (verse 1). In verse 5, the people who insisted on retaining circumcision as a condition of salvation were identified as "believers who belonged to the party of the Pharisees."

Try to understand the problem from the viewpoint of the Pharisees. These people had taken a monumental step away from the religion of their forefathers in the act of turning to Jesus. They had probably endured criticism, ostracism, and family rejection as the result of their decision to embrace the Christian faith.

Their cultural conditioning had led them to believe that God deals with the human race only through the nation of Israel. About the time they became reconciled to the revolutionary idea of being followers of Jesus, Peter showed up and said that God had directed him to the house of Cornelius for the purpose of proclaiming God's redemptive program to the Gentiles. That within itself was hard to take, but then right on the heels of Peter's shocking change of direction came Paul and the Gentile evangelism program. Reluctantly, they had swallowed each bitter pill. Now they were being asked to take one more step; forget about circumcising the Gentile converts. That was just too much to take.

These people had trouble understanding that God was dealing with the human race in a fundamentally different way than they had previously understood. The elimination of the circumcision requirement was almost incidental to the program being presented. God was eliminating law as the basis of salvation.

A person who tends to think legalistically is quite willing to concede that the law of Moses has been abrogated. To him, the change means that the law of Moses has been replaced by the law of Christ. He fails to perceive that the law of Moses serves to illustrate the inability of law—any law—to make people righteous. There was nothing wrong with the law of Moses as a legal system. Paul conceded in Galatians 3:21, "Is the law, therefore, opposed to the promises of God? Absolutely not! For if a law had been given that could impart life, then righteousness would certainly have come by the law."

2. *Legalism thrives on guilt.* We are freed from the burden of sin through the grace of God. Jesus invited the human race to unburden itself when He said, "Come to me, all you who are weary and burdened, and I will give you rest. Take my yoke upon you and learn from me, for I am gentle and humble in heart, and you will find rest for your souls. For my yoke is easy and my burden is light" (Matthew 11:28-30). That's light years away from the emphasis of the legalist who says, "You're a Christian now. You're going to have to shape up. It's time for you to get your act together. If you don't get it together pretty soon, you're going to be in big trouble with the Lord because you're like the dog that has turned to his own vomit and the sow that has turned to wallowing in the mire."

Many sensitive and guilt-ridden Christians have been robbed of their joy by that kind of abrasive approach. They grow up under an incessant barrage of legalistic teaching and find it hard to let go of old guilt feelings, even after they have intellectually accepted God's program of grace. Many of us will find ourselves agreeing with the comment of Lloyd John Ogilvie: "Long after we are set free in Christ, the old memory tapes are replayed with guilt producing regularity."[7]

3. *Legalism transforms tradition into law.* Making laws out of tradition has plagued Christianity from its very beginning. When the Pharisees questioned Jesus about the failure of His disciples to observe the traditional handwashing rituals, He asked, "And why do you break the command of God for the sake of your tradition?" (Matthew 15:3). The Colossian heresy included a set of rigid traditionalized forms. Paul wrote, "See to it that no one takes you captive through hollow and deceptive philosophy, which depends on human tradition and the basic principles of this world rather than on Christ" (Colossians 2:8).

David Chadwell suggests that "a serious problem of modern Pharisaism exists in the Lord's church. It binds human judgments on Christians by demanding conformity to accepted interpretations."[8] Although we pride ourselves on having "no creed but Christ," the fact is that we have developed many traditions within our fellowship that have become all but set in granite; these traditions amount to an unwritten creed. The sad part of it all is that Christ has very little part in our creed.

The binding of human tradition can be observed in many different settings in the contemporary church. Joe Baisden of Belton, Texas, tells a rather bizarre story of how misunderstanding coupled with devotion to tradition created near panic in a church where he once ministered. A man, who at that point was not a member of the church, owned a vineyard. He thought it would be a nice gesture to donate grape juice from his vineyard for the communion service. The elders of the church accepted the man's generous offer, but failed to announce to the congregation that there would be a change in grape juice suppliers. The juice from the donor's vineyard turned out to be slightly different in color from the store-bought variety. Many members of the church were highly offended; some even refused to come back to services on Sunday night. The elders were accused of introducing Kool-Aid in the communion service and were pressed to produce biblical authority for such a practice.

Isn't it strange how we have come to accept a certain commercially prepared fruit of the vine as the only acceptable means of commemorating the shed blood of our Savior? I wonder how many of us would be willing to accept white grape juice in the communion. In American Restoration churches, fermented wine is almost never used in communion, but in other cultures it is quite common. I'll never forget the sense of shock I felt the first time I attended a worship service in which fermented wine was served in communion. I didn't think it was wrong, but I hadn't been culturally prepared to accept it. Seldom do we stop to ponder the possibility that we've entrenched human tradition in our selection of which form of the fruit of the vine to use in the Lord's Supper.

Thomas Olbricht suggests that our attitude toward certain procedures indicates that we often transform tradition into a "law of God." He says, "Take for example the tenacity with which some cling to the King James Version, extending the invitation at the close of every service, or certain programs of activity for the church."[9]

Traditions nearly always develop as the result of human reasoning and then become firmly set as controversy arises from those who refuse to buy the traditional package. In the 1920s, church members fought the "bobbed hair" fad with great fierceness. "Bobbed hair" would scarcely raise a ripple of protest in the contemporary church. Fifty years later, however, the granddaughters of the ladies who first bobbed their hair found themselves locked in mortal combat over the propriety of wearing pantsuits to church services. That, too, has pretty well subsided in most areas. Nevertheless, traditions die hard, and there's nearly always someone who believes the Scriptures have been compromised when a cherished tradition is discarded.

During my youth, many preachers condemned the practice of attending the movies. All movies were on the forbidden list—those featuring Gene Autry, Roy Rogers, or cartoons were considered just as wrong as those starring Tyrone Power, Clark Gable, or Jane Russell. Their argument was that attending a movie classified one as a moviegoer. In their view, the public wouldn't be intelligent enough to know whether one only went to Gene Autry movies or not. They were certain that if others saw a member put his money down at the box office window, they would judge him as a person who would be attracted to the most lurid films Hollywood could offer. And that was pretty tame stuff compared to today's cinematic productions. Strangely enough, that entire line of reasoning changed the moment television became popular, and television sets began to appear in the living rooms of those preachers.

Traditions vary from congregation to congregation and culture to culture. People who spend their entire lives in one geographical area may not even be aware of the regional and cultural differences that are present in the church today. But as society becomes more mobile, the clash of differing traditions becomes more evident. We must recognize that the gospel isn't limited to the framework of a single culture and that the perspectives of any given region aren't necessarily the only true perspectives. What is needed is a more cosmopolitan view of the church, and that can take place only as we learn to separate tradition from revelation.

4. *Legalism makes the human response the essence of the gospel.* Therein lies the heresy of legalism. Too often we view the legalist as a harmless crank. For the sake of harmony we're willing to humor him, but the legalist is guilty of sin on at least two counts. In the first place, he arbitrarily sets limits on the freedom that Christ has given us to enjoy. When legalism threatened the churches of Galatia, Paul wrote to them, "It is for freedom that Christ has set us free. Stand firm, then, and do not let yourselves be burdened again by a yoke of slavery" (Galatians 5:1).

It's true that there comes a time when liberty must be surrendered for the sake of another person's soul. Paul says, "It is better not to eat meat or drink wine or do anything else that will cause your brother to fall" (Romans 14:21). If a brother's soul were at stake, Paul advised the voluntary surrender of one's liberty. He was even willing to become a vegetarian and a total abstainer for the sake of a weak brother, although he maintained his liberty to eat meat and drink wine. On the other hand, he did not counsel the surrender of freedom for the sake of the power hungry legalist who wants to impose his will on the church. Power plays are to be resisted.

Second, the legalist is guilty of sin when he knowingly or unknowingly attempts to replace the work of Christ as our Savior with the work of man. To view salvation as a work of human merit is to cheapen what was done on the cross.

> It is Christ who saves. Hence the conditions of salvation must relate to him. But they must relate to him as *sinbearer*, not as the mere *author* of the conditions of salvation. The conditions of salvation are responses to Jesus as "Lord and Christ" (Acts 2:36). Christ, not mere duty, is the consideration of salvation. This point is of utmost significance. It must be conceded or the cross is nullified.[10]

5. *Legalism equates human perception of the Word of God with the Word of God itself.* The attraction of legalism is the overpowering sense of being right.

> In the preface of a Restoration Movement publication, a popular author sought to establish the credibility of his work by asserting that his arguments could not be answered. He expressed confidence that his polemics would prevail over any adversary.

The author most certainly can't be accused of ambivalence. He takes a definite stand, and he's absolutely convinced that he's right. Unfortunately, his affirmations tend to come across to others as harsh and egocentric, whether he intended them to be taken that way or not.

No human being has a corner on all truth. God hasn't endowed any person in the church with the blessing of infallibility. Debates usually create more heat than light and feed the ego needs of the ones doing the debating. Truth tends to get buried beneath the power struggle going on among antagonists.

6. *Legalism produces a divisive spirit.* Legalists are never able to agree with one another. When a difference of interpretation arises, legalists square off against one another in a battle royal, which usually ends in everyone choosing up sides and going their separate ways.

When the Restoration Movement flowered on the American church scene in the nineteenth century, it offered the promise of bringing men together under the banner of Christ. Protestantism really didn't show all that much interest in unity during the nineteenth century. If we have any thought of serving as a catalyst for unity in today's world, we must realize that our own credibility has been severely damaged by our inability to practice the unity for which we plead. Our heritage has been marred by sectarian practices and divisions even as we claim to abhor sectarianism.

7. *Legalism makes a long list of demands, but offers no power to live up to them.* In the Foreword, I related the story of a woman who came into my office questioning her salvation. Consider her plight. In her youth, she took her relationship with God very seriously. She went to Bible class regularly. She usually knew her memory verse and would be the first one to answer questions in class. Her conduct in terms of personal morality was commendable. Cigarettes didn't touch her lips. She wouldn't have known the difference between a whiskey sour and a martini because she didn't drink anything that contained alcohol. Profane words weren't in her vocabulary. She had been taught to avoid the appearance of evil. She tried her best to do just that. Still, she knew that her life had some imperfections in it—bad thoughts, neglected duties, conflicts in personal relationships for which she had to share at least some of the blame. She wanted to live a

better life, but up to that point she hadn't been able to muster enough strength to measure up to her ideals. Thus, even though she understood grace from an intellectual point of view, it was so foreign to the teaching of her childhood that she couldn't bring herself to accept it emotionally. She felt condemned.

Perhaps it was her intellectual understanding of grace that kept her coming back to church. However, many people who don't understand grace but do understand responsibility have concluded that Christianity is just too hard to live up to. Having decided that God's lists of demands are too long and too impractical, they walk right out of the church and away from God. You may well know individuals like that.

Love, the Alternative to Legalism

Former students of R. C. Bell, who taught Bible at Abilene Christian College for more than twenty-five years, remember him saying, "Young people, love God and do what you please." If that sounds permissive at the first reading, one must remember that the key is to truly love God. When Bell set his thoughts down on paper, he explained it this way,

> Law can make subjects and slaves, but it cannot soften hearts, break stubborn wills and generate gratitude and love, as grace does. That his plea for Christian living may be effective, Paul roots it in divine grace, not in law and the will of the flesh. To lift men out of sin, they must be brought into a realm where grace, not law, is the constitution. Law and fear are not comparable to grace and gratitude in the power to purify.[11]

Paul saw himself so closely identified with Christ that he said, "I have been crucified with Christ and I no longer live, but Christ lives in me" (Galatians 2:20). A person can love God and then do what he pleases because loving God with all one's heart, mind, and soul means that person loves what God loves. It's impossible to imagine a lover of God deliberately setting out to do what will break God's heart.

The Scriptures speak clearly on this matter. Concerning the responsibility to love God and love people, Jesus said, "All the Law and the Prophets hang on these two commandments" (Matthew 22:40). Paul wrote, "He who loves his fellowman has fulfilled the law" (Romans 13:8), and he made the same point in stronger language in Galatians 5:14: "The *entire* law is summed up in a single command: 'Love your neighbor as yourself' " (emphasis added). Bell observed, "Christians do not need to be under law to be lawful. . . . Love does not disregard it, but on her magical feet, she outruns law on her leaden feet, and does the good deed before the law arrives."[12]

The ethical requirements of the Bible are intended to teach us how to love. In Colossians 3, Paul gave a rather lengthy list of moral exhortations urging his readers to avoid sexual immorality, lust, greed, and other sins. Then he named some positive traits and tied the whole thing back to the principle of love: "And over all these virtues put on love, which binds them all together in perfect unity" (Colossians 3:14). That differs significantly from viewing biblical ethics as a checklist of requirements that a person must meet in order to qualify for entrance to heaven.

Summary and Conclusion

Legalism has one thing in common with taxes, fleas, and ticks—it has always been around. Even those who like to deny their legalism often display certain legalistic tendencies. Legalism is a rather difficult word to define because most of us tend to use the term to describe any position that is to the right of what we have chosen to believe. In any kind of objective consideration of the subject, individuals need to concentrate more on identifying characteristics than attempting to compose a textbook definition.

Legalism reduces Christianity to mere rule keeping. It's more of an emphasis than an identifiable position. The grace-oriented person is no less interested in complete adherence to Scripture than the legalist. But he seeks to know the will of God in order to understand how to better love God rather than to be able to touch all the mandatory bases prescribed by divine law. The demands of Christianity are powered by love, not by coercion and threat.

> Love so amazing, So divine
> Demands my soul, my life, my all.
> —Isaac Watts

Thought Questions

1. Why do we all demonstrate legalistic tendencies?
2. What is the difference between biblical obedience and legalistic obedience?
3. What are the weaknesses of legalism as a justifying principle?

4. What was the basic flaw in the law of Moses?
5. How can we rid ourselves of the guilt brought on by long exposure to legalistic instruction?
6. Why do we tend to transform tradition into law?
7. What are some of the traditions we maintain in the church as if they were part of the gospel?
8. What is the primary error of making the human response to Christ the essence of the gospel?
9. Why do men tend to equate their perception of the Word with the Word itself?
10. How can we teach people that love is the only law God has without encouraging them to view love as a license to sin?

Notes

[1]Joseph C. Aldrich, *Lifestyle Evangelism* (Portland, Ore.: Multnomah Press, 1981), p. 131.

[2]Henry Bosley Woulf, editor in chief, *Webster's New Collegiate Dictionary* (Springfield, Mass.: G. and C. Merriam and Co., 1977), p. 656.

[3]Thomas Olbricht, "Legalism Today," *Firm Foundation*, September 17, 1963.

[4]Monroe Hawley, *The Focus of Our Faith* (Nashville, Tenn.: Twentieth Century Christian, 1985), pp. 127-28.

[5]David Chadwell, *Beware of the Leaven of the Pharisees* (Abilene, Tex.: Quality Publications, 1985), pp. 58-59.

[6]K. C. Moser, *The Gist of Romans* (Oklahoma City: privately published, 1958), p. x.

[7]Lloyd John Ogilvie, *Loved and Forgiven* (Ventura, Calif.: Regal Books, 1977), p. 88.

[8]Chadwell, *Beware of the Leaven of the Pharisees*, p. 74.

[9]Olbricht, *"Legalism Today."*

[10]Moser, *The Gist of Romans*, p. x.

[11]R. C. Bell, *Studies in Romans* (Austin, Tex.: Firm Foundation Publishing House, 1957), p. 55.

[12]Ibid., p. 152.

C H A P T E R 9

The Spirit and the Letter

During the administration of Thomas Jefferson, the purchase of the Louisiana Territory from France became a live option for the federal government. Jefferson favored a "strict constructionist" approach to constitutional law, which meant he believed the government must have definite constitutional authority before it can act. The Constitution did not specifically authorize the government to purchase territory. On the other hand, how could the government afford to turn down the opportunity to double the size of its territory at the incredibly low price of $15 million?

Jefferson and the Congress resolved the dilemma by claiming the intent of the Constitution extended to the purchase of property. The key element in their interpretation was the clause empowering Congress "to provide for the common defence and general welfare of the United States." They reasoned that control of the Mississippi River would contribute to the national defense. Some of Jefferson's opponents were quick to point out his inconsistencies. Nevertheless, his reasoning prevailed with the Congress. Those who favored the Louisiana Purchase contended that the spirit of the Constitution overrode the letter.[1]

As restorationists, we struggle with Jefferson's dilemma in our search for a viable hermeneutic. Legalism remains popular in restoration churches because many of us are strict constructionists who view the New Testament as a mere law document. In *The Declaration and Address*, Thomas Campbell described the New Testament as a "constitution" for the church.[2] Such an unfortunate choice of terms has contributed to an atmosphere in which the letter has received far more emphasis than the spirit. When the New Testament is reduced to codified law, hostility and strife are the inevitable consequences. Restoration history indicates that it also leaves behind a residue of division.

When Christians come to understand that they are saved by grace, they will find it necessary to wrestle with the tensions between the letter and the spirit. This doesn't mean that Christians can afford to forget about conforming to New Testament patterns; the Bible does include obligatory statements. But if we are expected to obey biblical commands, how do we go about deciding which ones are manifestations of the first-century culture and which ones are transcultural? If the New Testament does indeed mandate permanent patterns of behavior, how detailed are those patterns? How much latitude is left to Christians who operate through a different cultural perspective, in a different time frame, at a different level of formal academic training?

It would be unrealistic to suggest that all hermeneutical differences among restorationists could be resolved by a proper understanding of spirit and letter considerations. It would be naive to suggest that all our problems and divisions stem from a faulty viewpoint in these areas. Nevertheless, if we would be really serious about making meaningful progress toward unity, we must come to grips with these issues.

Across the spectrum of religious thought, significant differences exist concerning what use to make of the Bible. At one end of the spectrum are those who assume that the New Testament doesn't contain any permanent, obligatory requirements. At the opposite end are those who reduce the Bible to a rule book.

No one can take the Bible seriously without recognizing that it requires certain standards of behavior, mandates the development of loving attitudes, and even imposes certain forms of response to God, such as baptism and the Lord's Supper. The problem lies in trying to decide how much human flexibility is allowed in the process of fulfilling biblical obligations.

Sometimes we have a tendency to read our own attitudes and temperamental characteristics into the Bible. An issue-oriented person who tends toward rigidity in his personality is often quite inflexible in his view of Scripture. Such a person insists that he's right, and he's not apt to be moved by any attempts to persuade him otherwise. His views were set in concrete a long time ago. An unstructured person with a permissive personality tends to look upon commands as threats to his freedom. But our hermeneutical options aren't limited to the choice between a blueprint on the one hand and loose guidelines on the other. There are many alternatives, and our challenge is to determine the degree of rigidity inherent in the New Testament patterns. Monroe Hawley has suggested that the synonyms for *pattern* indicate varying degrees of flexibility:

> If the New Testament gives a *guideline* for Christians, this might imply little more than a direction to be followed. *Model, example* and *standard* suggest something more specific. *Blueprint* on the other

hand, usually implies a pattern with all the details worked out.[3]

Perhaps persons who want to eliminate the pattern concept are really disenchanted with the blueprint approach. In the final analysis, the extent to which the details of New Testament forms are to be retained must be worked out by determining the *intent* of the original writers of Scripture.

The Limitations of Law

In 1985, the Iowa legislature passed a law prohibiting persons to possess an alcoholic beverage in an open container while riding in an automobile. Unfortunately, the good intentions of the legislators were thwarted by a glitch in the wording. They forgot to define wine as an alcoholic drink. Although the 1986 legislative session produced an amendment to correct this oversight, one could actually drive and legally drink wine from an open container in Iowa for an entire year.

A similar problem with the law came to light during the Iran-Contra hearings in 1987. Some members of the legal profession contended that the much-heralded Boland amendment, which prohibited the executive branch of government from entering into agreements without informing Congress, did not apply to the National Security Council because the law neglected to mention that agency by name.

In both instances, either law or the interpretation of law became a frustration to legislative bodies because they intended one thing while law said something else. These recent legal snags illustrate the inherent limitation of any kind of law structure. Law, by its very nature, simply can't take into account the entire range of human variables.

Although the Bible contains propositional truth, which includes commands to be obeyed, people who regard it as the spiritual equivalent of secular law misunderstand its purpose. Much of the divisiveness that has haunted the American Restoration Movement is rooted in the legal mentality that has often guided the movement. It's unfortunate that the spirit of Blackstone has guided some of our polemicists more than the spirit of Christ.

The law approach to Scripture is inadequate because those who urge the church to think in terms of legality often *appropriate the Bible for uses that God never intended.* Although behavior requirements, attitude expectations, and outward forms of response are indeed mandated by Scripture, the Bible is essentially a story. It's a story about God's love for man and His unbroken determination to rescue fallen members of the human race who have allowed themselves to become alienated from fellowship with Him. The story centers in a Person. Paul could argue with the craftiest legal technicians of his day, but he concentrated on a Christ-centered message: "For I resolved to know nothing while I was with you except Jesus Christ and him crucified" (1 Corinthians 2:2). When the Ethiopian eunuch inquired about the interpretation of an Old Testament passage that had long engaged the Jewish rabbis in vigorous debate, Philip declined to enter the arena of polemics. Instead, he "began with that very passage of Scripture and told him the good news about Jesus" (Acts 8:35).

The law approach is suspect because it *encourages the dishonest practice of prooftexting.* A good "prooftexting"

preacher can manage to work in thirty or forty discon-
nected passages in a single sermon. If he has devoted
some of his energy to memory work, he can dazzle the
audience with his performance, and people will go away
marveling at his great command of the Scriptures. As
he layers text on top of text in support of his premises,
he can become persuasive to those who never bother to
check the context from which those references have been
taken. Prooftexting is dishonest and manipulative when
it ignores the contextual and historical setting of the
passage.

In my library, I have a book that does this very thing.
Literally hundreds of Bible references are cited by the
author in a book that runs about two hundred pages.
There's a lot of Bible in it, but there's very little truth.
The book espouses Jehovah's Witness theology. As restorationists, we compromise our integrity when we indict
people of various denominational persuasions for distort-
ing the Scriptures by ignoring context and then do the
same thing ourselves.

The law approach *doesn't consider the intent of Scripture.*
When I was a teenager, our teacher used to ask the
members of our high-school Bible class to take turns
reading a section of Scripture, after which we were
expected to make some sort of comment. If we had any
trouble coming up with something intelligent, we soon
learned to say, "It just means what it says." The teacher
always let us get away with that! It was our way of putting
the ball back into his court.

We had been taught that the truth is so plain that "the
wayfaring men though fools should not err therein." To
us, the statement meant the Bible is just as plain as the
nose on your face, and it doesn't need any human

commentary to enhance its understanding. Of course we never stopped to think that if the Bible were really all that simple, we wouldn't have needed Bible school teachers or preachers. Besides that, we never bothered to check the prooftext in Isaiah, or we would have quickly learned that our mentors had misapplied that one.

While Scripture does "mean just what it says," sometimes a great deal of mental industry is required just to figure out what it actually says. Even Peter, who was an inspired writer, conceded that his fellow apostle, Paul, had written some things that were hard to understand (see 2 Peter 3:16).

The apostle Paul insisted that the spirit of the Word outweighed the letter. In Romans 2:28-29, he said, "For he is not a Jew which is one outwardly; neither is that circumcision which is outward in the flesh; But he is a Jew which is one inwardly; and circumcision is that of the heart, in the spirit, and not in the letter; whose praise is not of men, but of God" (KJV). What did Paul mean when he contrasted the Spirit with the written code? J. D. Thomas notes, "The expression 'in the spirit and not in the letter' here means that genuine spiritual dedication is required and not just a literal fleshly circumcision or 'labeling' as belonging to the Lord."[4]

This internalizing of the law is also emphasized in the Hebrew writer's quote from Jeremiah:

> I will make a new covenant
>   with the house of Israel. . . .
> It will not be like the covenant
>   I made with their forefathers. . . .
> I will put my laws in their minds

and write them on their hearts (Hebrews 8:8-10).

These passages suggest that there is more to understanding God's will for us than being able to list the external commands of the Bible. We need to know *why* God has issued a command. He explains Himself; He reveals His nature through His Son; He opens up His purpose in the world through the biblical story. To comprehend the will of God, we must move beyond mere law to comprehend the divine intent.

The gospel is not to be viewed as a streamlined version of the law of Moses. The gospel tells a new and different story about how unrighteous people are permitted to wear the clothing of righteousness. That's grace. Law can justify people only through their perfect performance. Grace justifies people through Christ's perfect performance.

Determining the Intent of Scripture

In his novel *Catch-22*, Joseph Heller tells the story of an American soldier who sets out to gain a discharge from the army by pretending to be crazy. He substantiates his claim only to learn he can't obtain a discharge on that basis because he's smart enough to figure out he's crazy. If he's that smart, he's rational enough to serve in the army. After all, everything the army does is crazy. This tongue-in-cheek novel became so popular that "Catch-22" came to be applied to any kind of order, command, or instruction that causes a person to disobey another instruction when he complies with the original one.

If we view the Scriptures as mere law, then we're led to the inescapable conclusion that some Bible commands fall into the Catch-22 category. According to Joshua 2:4-5, Rahab disobeyed God's command about bearing false witness when she lied about the whereabouts of the Hebrew spies. Did she lie with God's approval? In Hebrews 11:31, she was honored as a heroine of the faith because she welcomed the spies. According to Matthew 12:3-4, David disobeyed the Old Testament law that prohibited eating consecrated bread. Jesus condoned David's practice and defended His own action, giving David's example as a precedent.

Lest one should think all the Catch-22's are confined to the long distant past, consider the following dilemmas. A Christian leaves his home with the intent of attending the assembly in obedience to Hebrews 10:25. On his way to church, he passes by an accident where a motorist has been severely injured. Should he stop and render aid? The love principle says he should. But which command does he obey? A Christian woman is married to an unbeliever. According to Scripture, she is to win her husband through her quiet and submissive demeanor, but what does she do when her husband orders her to stay away from church services? One doesn't have to dream up imaginary events to discover spiritually sensitive people trapped in ethical dilemmas. They happen regularly in most congregations.

These conflicts can be resolved by focusing on the *intent* of God's commands. When Paul speaks of a person becoming an "inward Jew," he's pointing out the fact that the Word of God concentrates more on matters of the heart than on forms. But how are we to discern the intent of the message? How are we to know if we have correctly determined the intent of the things God has spoken in Scripture? Although they certainly do not contain authoritative answers, the following guidelines suggest a practical way to discern God's intent.

1. *Matters that affect the heart must take precedence over form, structure, and ritual.* Jesus indicted the Pharisees because they had meticulously bound the tithing law on the Jews and ignored the "more important matters of the law" (Matthew 23:23). Among those qualities, He included justice, mercy, and faithfulness as characteristics of the inward man. Tithing one's vegetables from the garden involved external concerns.

2. *When our interpretation of the letter causes us to brutalize, manipulate, or abuse people, we have misunderstood the intent of the message.* Thomas Aquinas was so zealous for his understanding of right forms and doctrines that he thought adherence to them ought to take precedence over the humane treatment of people. Concerning heretics, he said, "There is sin, whereby they deserve not only to be separated from the church by excommunication, but also to be shut off from the world by death."[5] Modern secular law is far too tolerant to allow Aquinas's solution to the heresy problem to be practiced. One does wonder, however, what horrors might be inflicted on the population if some legalists were to have their way. In Paul's letter to the church at Corinth, he indicated that the overriding principle that guides the Christian in choosing his response to people is his concern for the personhood of those who have been created in God's image. He says, "Do everything in love" (1 Corinthians 16:14).

3. *Our conclusions must match the total expression of God's will in the New Testament.* In John 8, the accusers of Jesus tried to trap Him in a dichotomy between His respect for the law and His commitment to personhood.

The law said, "Stone the woman! She's an adulteress!" Compassion said, "Forgive the woman! She's been victimized by the tempter!" Jesus chose compassion when He said to her, "Go now and leave your life of sin" (John 8:11). Jesus wasn't soft on the adultery command, but He viewed the seventh commandment in the light of God's desire to forgive. Someone has said, "Confrontation without compassion is brutality, while compassion without confrontation is sentimentality."

4. *We must understand that the Bible is a story about Jesus.* If our interpretation of Scripture leads us away from Christ, we have misunderstood the language of Scripture, even though we may have consulted lexicons, grammars, commentaries, and the finest tools of contemporary scholarship before reaching our conclusions. We must keep in mind Paul's words: "I want to know Christ and the power of his resurrection and the fellowship of sharing in his sufferings, becoming like him in his death" (Philippians 3:10).

An apocryphal story about Karl Barth helps us to come to grips with matters of faith that count the most. Supposedly, the theologian was asked to identify the most profound thought that had come to his attention in his many years of theological studies. He was reputed to have replied, "Jesus loves me, this I know, for the Bible tells me so."

The Bible wasn't written to fuel debates between warring factions of the church. It wasn't written to give power hungry men an opportunity to control and manipulate people. It wasn't designed as a whip to be used to force people to align themselves with a certain viewpoint. A person may wave his Bible and quote enough Scripture to overwhelm his listener, but his approach is out of focus if his focus isn't on Jesus.

We'll never come to a meeting of the minds by arguing our way to agreement on all the details of the human response to the Bible. Debaters have a way of saying nice things about open-mindedness and their willingness to participate in a truth search, but in debate, human ego often gets in the way of the truth search. When a person throws down the gauntlet and challenges another person with a differing view to debate, he usually has every intention of winning the contest, and he gets charged up with just as much adrenaline as an athlete does on the playing field. Too often the truth search gets abandoned in the process.

A legalistic approach to Christianity results in nitpicking. A libertarian approach ends up in license. Our task as Christians is to determine the *intent* of God's message. If we can see Scripture as a heart-directed message, then we've got a chance to achieve some of the noble objectives the restoration pioneers dreamed about in the nineteenth century.

Summary and Conclusion

Restorationists struggle with tensions between the letter of biblical commands and the intent behind those commands. Viewing the New Testament merely as a document of law leaves us open to a type of legalism that encourages hostility and religious division. Although legalism is to be abhorred, the opposite extreme of antinomianism produces an unhealthy atmosphere of religious permissiveness. Thoughtful Christians need to concentrate on developing a hermeneutic that recaptures the original intent of the biblical writers.

Our search for a viable hermeneutic requires unbiased objectivity as we attempt to separate the cultural material of the Bible from the transcultural principles. Such an approach to biblical study will lead us to the conclusion that the Bible does indeed contain propositional truth, but we must stop short of seeing it as a law document. The law approach to the study of Scripture is inadequate because it subverts the Bible's intended purpose, it encourages the dishonest practice of prooftexting, and it doesn't take the intent of Scripture into consideration.

Perhaps the most difficult exercise in coming to grips with an adequate hermeneutic is that of developing objective guidelines for determining the intent of Scripture. In this chapter, four principles have been offered as criteria for determining the intent of the biblical authors: (1) matters of the heart take precedence over form, structure, and ritual; (2) when an interpretation brutalizes, manipulates, or abuses people, that interpretation must be considered as a misunderstanding of Scripture's intent; (3) conclusions must match the total expression of God's will in the New Testament; and (4) the Bible must be seen as a story about Jesus.

In many ways, restorationists are confronted with the necessity of reconsidering cherished and accepted traditions if these principles are followed. The temptation to affirm extreme viewpoints is ever present. When the Bible is viewed solely as a law document, the spirit of servanthood loses out to legalistic nit-picking. When antinomianism is the standard, people tend to become slaves of their own self-seeking attitudes, conforming to scriptural standards only when it suits their pleasure. The objective student of Scripture asks, "What is God saying to me about how He wants me to run my life."

Thought Questions

1. In what way does Jefferson's constitutional dilemma over the Louisiana Purchase parallel our own problems in biblical interpretation?
2. How can we separate the cultural material of the Bible from the transcultural?
3. What is meant by "spirit" and "letter?"
4. How does the hermeneutic principle of studying to determine the intent of Scripture relate to grace?
5. What's the difference between a pattern and a blueprint?
6. What are the major fallacies of viewing the New Testament as mere law?
7. What is the primary purpose of the Bible?
8. Why do matters of the heart take precedence over matters of form?
9. How does the debating mentality dim our view of Jesus?
10. What additional guidelines would you suggest for determining the intent of the biblical writers?

Notes

[1]Thomas James Norton, *The Constitution of the United States—Its Sources and Applications* (Cleveland: World Publishing, 1941), pp. 80-81.

[2]Thomas Campbell, *The Declaration and Address*, quoted by James DeForest Murch, *Christians Only* (Cincinnati: Standard Publishing, 1962), p. 45.

[3]Monroe E. Hawley, *The Focus of Our Faith* (Nashville, Tenn.: Twentieth Century Christian, 1985), p. 117.

[4]J. D. Thomas, *Romans* (Austin, Tex.: R. B. Sweet Co., 1965), p. 30.

[5]Thomas Aquinas *Summa Theologica* ii, Q. xi, art. iii-iv, quoted by Henry Bettenson, *Documents of the Christian Church* (New York and London: Oxford University Press, 1947), pp. 189-90.

Cheap Grace

In the years since World War II, the expression *cheap grace* has often been associated with the name of Dietrich Bonhoeffer. Born into an aristocratic German family early in the twentieth century, Bonhoeffer bordered on academic genius. By the time he reached manhood, National Socialism was poised to seize control of Germany's government. He considered Hitler's movement to be a malignant, destructive social force that couldn't be reconciled with the historic Christian faith.

Bonhoeffer was aligned with the "confessing church"—the portion of German Lutheranism that Berlin tried to suppress. He became an underground resistance worker and ultimately participated in the abortive attempt to assassinate Hitler in the summer of 1944. He was arrested, and shortly before the close of the war, he was hanged on orders from Heinrich Himmler.

In 1937, he published *The Cost of Discipleship*. The book, which is still in print, is really a critical appraisal of official German Lutheranism during the Nazi years. The German clerics had reasoned, "We are powerless to do anything about the Third Reich. Our task is a spiritual one. We don't see ourselves as agents of social and political change, so we must accommodate ourselves to the political realities that exist. It's our business to make the best of the situation and go on conducting church work as usual." To Bonhoeffer, this rationalization was not only naive; it represented a denial of the church's mission in the world. In angry reaction he wrote, "Cheap grace is the deadly enemy of the church. We are fighting today for costly grace."[1]

The permissive moral and spiritual atmosphere of the late twentieth century compels us to summon the moral courage to echo Bonhoeffer's sentiment. The cheap grace partisans are still around, advising us to accommodate ourselves to the social and moral realities of contemporary culture. People would like to be thought of as good Christians without having to adhere to any moral and spiritual restraints. The closing line of the book of Judges could well be written as the epitaph for the church as it exists in some areas: "Everyone did as he saw fit" (Judges 21:25).

The Concept of Optional Obedience

Cheap grace thinking all but eliminates obedience as a spiritual requirement in human lives. Such terms as *essential, obligatory,* and *required* have been studiously excluded from the vocabulary of many contemporary religious spokespersons. Within the Churches of Christ, we seem to find ourselves in an era when we yearn for more exposure to the loving side of God's nature. This hunger is especially keen among persons whose entire religious experience has been legalistic and issue oriented. It's impossible to fault such noble desires. Nevertheless, a word of caution is in order. We must understand that love and sentimentality aren't the same thing. There's a tough side to love. There are times when love requires some things we'd rather not do. We must remember the

Lord's words to the church in Laodicea: "Those whom I love I rebuke and discipline" (Revelation 3:19).

The concept of optional obedience is not a recent phenomenon. In the context of church history, it goes back to the middle of the second century and the rise of monasticism. As the social makeup of the church gradually shifted from those who had been converted out of the world to those who were Christians as the result of their heritage, the attitude developed that the standards of Christianity were beyond the reach of the rank and file. People who were serious about obeying God entered the monasteries where they were encouraged to live an ascetic life that separated them from the contamination of a perverted world. Consequently, obedience became optional. If you wanted to be obedient, you entered the monastery. Otherwise, you went to church on Sunday and pretty much lived like other men the rest of the time.

There were two problems with the monastic life. (1) The monastics thought they could get closer to God by separating themselves from people. But they failed to see that God's purposes for the human race weren't served by withdrawing from the world. Jesus prayed, "My prayer is not that you take them out of the world but that you protect them from the evil one" (John 17:15). (2) The monastics were wrong in thinking that obedience was limited to the select few. Nowhere does the Word of God suggest that church members may elect a lifestyle of self-indulgence. There are no rankings in the kingdom of heaven. The clergy-laity distinction simply cannot be found in Scripture.[2]

The entire church falls under the mandate of Titus 2:11-12: "For the grace of God that brings salvation has appeared to all men. It teaches us to say 'No' to ungodliness and worldly passions, and to live self-controlled, upright and godly lives in this present age." The cheap grace revised version might read, "The grace of God has appeared, teaching us that it is permissible to indulge our passions without feeling guilt and to live undisciplined, indulgent, and self-centered lifestyles, for God does not want to inhibit our pleasure in this present age."

The seeds of cheap grace are planted in fertile soil in any religious group that allows legalism to dominate the thinking and the life of the church. Church members who spend years in the stifling atmosphere of rigid control by the self-appointed protectors of orthodoxy grow weary of living in a guilt-ridden atmosphere. Legalism has a way of spawning power brokers, and Christians who maintain even the tiniest bit of personal independence resent the attempts at manipulation. This explains why some members of the church who were once leading the fight for orthodoxy have lapsed into unbelief. To others who aren't ready to jettison the faith, the option looks very attractive when cheap grace theology is presented.

While one sympathizes with the person who has grown weary of legalism's heavy burdens, the fact remains that obedience is a part of the grace program. There is as much difference between biblical obedience and legalistic rule keeping as there is between apples and oranges. Legalism thrives on guilt and fear. Obedience, from the biblical perspective, is a response to love. Legalism concentrates on minimal standards. In our fellowship, the Sunday night assembly rarely attracts the same number of people as the Sunday morning assembly. There are several explanations for this, but one reason is that many people don't think the Sunday night assembly is essential. They are interested in meeting minimal standards. Biblical obedience, on the other hand, isn't concerned about minimal standards. The question is not, "How much do I have to do?" but "How much is it possible for me to do?" Legalism is man centered; the emphasis is on human performance. Biblical obedience is Christ centered; the emphasis is on responding to Jesus.

Legalists inevitably make laws of their own, but they don't think of their actions as creating creeds. They just want to protect the church. Certain churches have devised questionnaires that all prospective teachers and preachers must be able to pass before they'll be allowed to give instruction. Quite often the questions are not based on a knowledge of Scripture, but on the inferences that certain people have drawn from Scripture. In this way, church leaders have made up human laws for the church just as certainly as some denominationalists have made up laws for their churches when they write human creeds.

Since biblical obedience doesn't thrive on guilt and fear, there is no need to erect artificial protective barriers. The same love that frees us from sin moves us to obey God: "This is love for God: to obey his commands. And his commands are not burdensome" (1 John 5:3). A person who truly loves God isn't going to engage in morally debased conduct. Furthermore, he will not deliberately and knowingly advocate doctrinal positions in conflict with the Scriptures.

Cheap Grace and Sin

The great fault of cheap grace is its tendency to

rationalize and justify disobedient behavior. At the same time, cheap grace develops a tolerance for false teaching. This cannot be healthy.

Human beings can be quite inventive when it comes to rationalizing beliefs and moral standards. One person reasons, "What I did or what I believe may be wrong, but given my set of circumstances and considering the way others have mistreated me, you must understand that I couldn't have reacted differently." He reasons that he's just a victim of circumstances. Because his circumstances have been so stressful, he wants God to make an exception in his case and expect less of him than He expects of other men.

Another person may reason, "What I did may not be altogether right, but you should have seen the party that went on at my neighbor's house last Saturday night. You would have thought my party was a Sunday school picnic in comparison." This form of rationalization enables a person to develop a ratings scale to determine the seriousness of sin. Let's say he rates the seriousness of sin on a scale of one to ten, with one being the least serious sin and ten being the most shocking thing he can imagine. He may feel rather smug about his own one or two rating when his neighbors are racking up eights and nines. To him, the seriousness of sin is a matter of degree. If he's not committing a really "bad" sin, then he doesn't have to be all that concerned about his spiritual condition.

Self-righteousness prevents the legalist from seeing his sin. He reasons, "I bring home my paycheck. I don't get drunk. I don't abuse my spouse. I worship every Sunday in a scripturally prescribed manner. I give at least 10 percent of my income to the church. I participate in the visitation program on Tuesday nights, I believe the right doctrines, and I attend only those seminars and lectures where sound brethren do the preaching." He's so wrapped up in his own goodness that he fails to take into account the personal sin that alienates him from God.

The Bible demands that we recognize the presence of sin in our lives. "For all have sinned and fall short of the glory of God" is the indictment of Romans 3:23. Roy H. Lanier asserts, "Nowhere in the Bible is man permitted to commit even one sin."[3] John forces us to the conclusion that sin must be confessed if it is to be forgiven: "If we claim to be without sin, we deceive ourselves and the truth is not in us. If we confess our sins, he is faithful and just and will forgive us our sins and purify us from all unrighteousness" (1 John 1:8-9).

To confess our sin is to see sin in the same light that God sees it. A confessing person will agree with God about his sin. It's a matter of personal honesty.

> Confession is not praying a lovely prayer or making a pious excuse or trying to impress God and other Christians. True confession is naming sin—calling it what God calls it: envy, lust, deceit or whatever it may be. Confession simply means being honest with ourselves and with God and if others are involved, being honest with them too. It is more than *admitting* sin. It means *judging* sin and facing it squarely.[4]

Nothing in the concept of grace allows us to view sin as an insignificant factor in our lives. Sin separates us from God. To claim forgiveness without any intention of obedience is to encourage a lifestyle of permissiveness. Bonhoeffer declared,

> Cheap grace is the preaching of forgiveness without requiring repentance, baptism without church discipline, communion without confession, absolution without personal confession. Cheap grace is grace without discipleship, grace without the cross, grace without Jesus Christ living and incarnate.[5]

There is no way to accept Jesus as our Savior without serving Him as Lord. Being disciples of Jesus still demands that we deny ourselves, take up the cross, and follow Him. Public opinion must never become the standard of obedience for Christians. It is a serious thing to rebel against the standards required by Scripture. To do so is to insult "the Spirit of grace" (Hebrews 10:29).

Part of the problem stems from a sociological aversion to sin, which has become a part of our national character. Our refusal to recognize sin's existence is well documented in *Whatever Became of Sin?* by Dr. Karl Menninger. He wrote, "In all the laments and reproaches made by our seers, one misses any mention of sin."[6]

John the Baptist wouldn't get much of a hearing in today's world. He could move into one of our major cities, trade in his camel's hair garment for a *Gentleman's Quarterly* approved wardrobe, and appear as a guest on the "Tonight Show" without attracting much attention. He would probably drive Johnny Carson's ratings down below those of the seventeenth rerun of "Gilligan's Island." John's demand to "produce fruit in keeping with repentance" (Matthew 3:8) wouldn't attract audiences in Los Angeles or New York. It wouldn't even play in Peoria, Platteville, Plainview, and Podunk. Why? Because we no longer care that much about sin.

The refusal to take sin seriously represents a major shift in our cultural values. Although much has been made of the skepticism that dominated the thinking of some of our founding fathers, the fact is that many of them were highly principled men with deep religious faith. One was Benjamin Rush, who worked tirelessly among the states to see that the Constitution was ratified. Rush was a physician and a founder of the American Psychiatric Association. He was also a militant moralist. He worked as hard to propagate his views on morality as he did to get the Constitution ratified. Among other things, he opposed county fairs (mainly because of their gambling activities), cock fighting, dining at men's clubs, and skating on Sunday.[7]

I grew up in an environment that Rush would have found very much to his liking. Preachers condemned some form of sin nearly every time they entered their pulpits. They didn't stop with the prohibitions of the Ten Commandments. They piled on the works of the flesh named in Galatians 5. Sometimes they would read between the lines and point out that things like dancing, mixed swimming, using tobacco, playing cards, and substituting bywords for profanity were to be considered as sins. Some of them condemned the movies. Even Gene Autry and Roy Rogers were considered off-limits for the person who was truly spiritually minded. Consumption of such beverages as tea, coffee, and carbonated drinks raised some eyebrows. I knew one person who claimed that a Christian should never drink root beer because "it is the very root of beer." Playing ball on Sundays was forbidden, and one suspected that it was probably sinful to laugh very loud or to admit that you enjoyed life. Joke telling was forbidden because the Scriptures said that we must give account for every idle word. (Honest, I'm not making any of this up.)

Maybe those fellows got carried away in their zeal to oppose "the appearance of evil," but they left little doubt concerning how they felt about sin. They were against it. If you were caught in violation of any of those taboos, there was a good chance you would hear about it in the next Sunday's sermon.

Today, we're afraid to label hardly anything a sin. It's just not in good taste. When the President of the United States proposed sexual abstinence as a solution to the AIDS problem, he was ridiculed by the pundits who wrote newspaper editorials. People began to suspect that he was an outdated relic of the past who didn't deserve to lead a nation in this century. Even in the church, the minister who sees one of his members commit a sin is well advised to turn his head the other way and keep his mouth shut. He most certainly will not bring the matter up in the Sunday morning sermon.

I am among the first to admit that some of the things I heard taught about morality during my youth were so unrealistic as to look ridiculous in the kind of world we live in now. They're not only outdated concepts; they won't stand the scrutiny of any objective evaluation. Our mentors had good intentions, but they were sometimes biased and judgmental. They manipulated the Scriptures and made them condemn everything they didn't like.

Enlightened minds chafe at that kind of demagoguery, but we must not allow ourselves to become so blasé about sin that we excuse it as acceptable behavior. God's grace is available to every sinner. That includes the murderer, the thief, the adulterer, the homosexual, and the pregnant teenager who gets an abortion. Even so, all of us must understand that forgiveness is only possible when we recognize our sin, repent of it, and let Jesus deal with it.

We must heed the truth in John's words: "My dear children, I write this to you so that you will not sin. But if anybody does sin, we have one who speaks to the Father in our defense—Jesus Christ, the Righteous One. He is the atoning sacrifice for our sins, and not only for ours but also for the sins of the whole world" (1 John 2:1-2).

Costly Grace

Bonhoeffer contrasted the popular idea of cheap grace with a concept he named *costly grace*. We must not think of the cost in terms of our being able to pay a price that would somehow qualify us for God's favor. It is a lifestyle of service offered to God in appreciation of His magnificent blessings. The compulsion to offer sacrifice to God comes as a natural result of understanding the nature of God's gift. The following are some appropriate responses to grace.

1. *Because of grace, we feel the compulsion to reorient our priorities.* In Matthew 13, Jesus compared the kingdom of heaven to a treasure hidden in a field. When the treasure hunter located the valuable object, he hid it again, "and then in his joy went and sold all he had and bought that field" (verse 44). The principle isn't hard to understand. The value of the kingdom is so precious that every other consideration is secondary. Anything the treasure hunter may be asked to give up is reasonable. The person who recognizes the supreme value of grace will not feel cheated because Jesus said, "No one who has left home or wife or brothers or parents or children for the sake of the kingdom of God will fail to receive

many times as much in this age and, in the age to come, eternal life" (Luke 18:29-30).

2. *Because of grace, we adopt a new set of thought patterns.* When Bonhoeffer first labeled National Socialism as an ungodly evil, most of the people of Germany didn't think Hitler was some kind of inhumane monster. His economic policies were beginning to pull the country out of the depression. The "Jewish" problem really didn't affect that many lives. Hitler's rise to power meant a return to prosperity. If the Jews came up short in the new arrangement of things, that was too bad, but they also had to understand economic reality.

Bonhoeffer swam against the tide of prevailing public opinion. Although his eventual decision to participate in the assassination plot is hard to square with Jesus' teachings, Bonhoeffer is to be admired for having the courage to place his life on the line rather than adjust his thinking to fit the requirements of a thoroughly evil power structure.

The sinner who is saved by grace no longer operates from the same frame of reference that controlled his thinking prior to becoming a Christian. Before Christ, the instinct for self-preservation, the desire to be catered to, and the desires of the flesh control a person's thought patterns. When that same person sees himself as an undeserving sinner who has been rescued from the enslavement of Satan and freed to live in the family of God, he takes on a new perspective concerning what's important in the world. It's from this point of view that Paul writes, "Set your minds on things above, not on earthly things" (Colossians 3:2).

3. *Because of grace, we will choose to follow Jesus even when we are asked to suffer.* On one occasion, an enthusias-

tic teacher of the law came out of the crowd and said, "Teacher, I will follow you wherever you go." Jesus replied, "Foxes have holes and birds of the air have nests, but the Son of Man has no place to lay his head" (Matthew 8:19-20).

It's not always going to be convenient to follow Jesus. For Paul, following Jesus meant beatings, stonings, shipwreck, physical dangers, imprisonment, attacks from false brethren in the church, hunger, thirst, cold, and insufficient clothing (see 2 Corinthians 11:23-29). Why was he willing to go through all that? The answer is found in 2 Corinthians 11:23: "Are they servants of Christ? (I am out of my mind to talk like this.) I am more." Because he had decided to become Christ's servant, he was willing to accept everything that went with that task—the Christian lifestyle, the attendant hardship, the revised way of thinking.

Today's church leaders are often concerned about indifference in the membership. They keep probing for ways to counteract materialism, apathy, and secularism. The problem can't be overcome by initiating cosmetic changes. New buildings, new specialized ministries, and good-looking, articulate ministers who can compete with the anchormen on the six o'clock news and adapt Madison Avenue marketing techniques won't turn the church around. A different attitude is needed. We'll never be able to turn things around with emotionally charged motivational speeches. As Vance Havner has noted, "There is something frightfully wrong when we have to beg most of the crowd to come to church to hear about it."[8] When we can see how much Christ has done for the church and internalize grace into our hearts,

Christ-like behavior will follow. It will be so intense that no power on earth can stop it.

Summary and Conclusion

Although he was certainly not the first to recognize the problem, Dietrich Bonhoeffer's response to the evils that prevailed throughout Hitler's Germany provided the framework for twentieth-century believers to better understand the difference between cheap grace and costly grace. Cheap grace is especially attractive to the comfort-oriented culture of the Western world. Cheap grace is the religion of optional obedience; it encourages us to slip into a pattern in which correct structures and forms in religion receive our attention while an appropriate response to Jesus from the inner being is neglected. When we understand that Christ not only set an example for us but also paid a price that we could not pay for ourselves, then love calls on us to emulate His example of servanthood. That's the exact opposite of the cheap grace approach that would like to plug into God's blessings without making a serious commitment.

The New Testament presents a view of grace in which a person's response to the magnificent outpouring of God's love is to live a life saturated with kingdom values. Because of grace, we will want to restructure our priorities, rework our thought patterns, and become willing to accept the suffering that comes with the kingdom.

> Take my life and let it be
> Consecrated, Lord, to thee:

Take my hands, and let them move
At the impulse of thy love.
                    —Frances E. Havergal

Thought Questions

1. Why is cheap grace the deadly enemy of the church?
2. To what extent have the Churches of Christ accepted the cheap grace philosophy?
3. What factors gave rise to the practice of monasticism?
4. How has legalism encouraged cheap grace?
5. What is the difference between biblical obedience and legalistic rule keeping?
6. Identify some ways Christians rationalize their sins.
7. What is confession?
8. Why has our culture developed an aversion to admitting the fact that sin occurs?
9. What motivates us to conduct ourselves toward Christ in the spirit of sacrifice?
10. List some difficulties we might expect to encounter when we truly follow Jesus.

Notes

[1]Dietrich Bonhoeffer, *The Cost of Discipleship* (New York: Macmillan, 1963), p. 45.

[2]For a discussion of the rise of monasticism, see Williston Walker, *A History of the Christian Church* (New York: Charles Scribners and Sons, 1918), pp. 102-5, 136-40.

[3]Roy H. Lanier, Sr., "Law and Grace," *Firm Foundation*, March 26, 1968.

[4]Warren Wiersbe, *Be Real* (Wheaton, Ill.: Victor Books, 1972), p. 38.

[5]Bonhoeffer, *Cost of Discipleship*, p. 47.

[6]Karl Menninger, *Whatever Became of Sin?* (New York: Hawthorne Books, 1978), p. 15.

[7]Ibid., p. 265.

[8]Vance Havner. *All or Nothing.* Church Bulletin, Jersey Village Church of Christ; Houston, TX. November 6, 1985.

C H A P T E R   1 1

Sanctification and Grace

It has been said that "anyone who tries to expound sanctification for discriminating readers should enter a plea for charity."[1] A person who sets out to write on the subject will never see his books on the shelves alongside those authored by Robert Ludlum and Louis L'Amour. Even serious-minded Christians back away from discussing sanctification.

Part of this aversion can be attributed to pure prejudice. I can still remember hearing derisive talk about the "sanctified folks" in the area where I was reared. The doctrinal soundness of any person who emphasized holiness was often considered suspect. Maybe that's because *sanctification* sounds a lot like *sanctimonious*. Actually, the two words aren't synonyms. *Sanctification* is "the act of sanctifying or making holy," but *sanctimonious* is "making a show of holiness."[2]

Most people, even most believers, aren't interested in the wars the theologians wage over the subject. They're quite willing to let bearded professors in tweed jackets battle over the sanctification issue behind the ivy-covered walls of the seminaries. They'd rather concentrate their attention on the real world of computers, cars, and cash.

Prejudice and indifference have something to do with our avoidance of serious study on the subject of sanctification, but I suspect that the real reason has something to do with our resistance to change. We're vaguely aware of the fact that God wants to change us. The thought of having to change something immediately triggers the braking mechanism in most human minds. We know enough about sanctification to understand that we're supposed to struggle with our habits, our behavior patterns, and our attitudes when they fall short of the Christ-like model. These changes are hard to make even when we acknowledge the presence of divine aid. Besides all that, grace-oriented people often doubt the motives of those who teach about sanctification. They fear being led back into the same old legalistic trap that once enslaved them. Jerry Bridges notes, "The concept of discipline is suspect in our society today. It appears counter to our emphasis on freedom in Christ and it often smacks of legalism and harshness."[3]

Scripture leads us to the conclusion, however, that all genuine Christians are in the process of sanctification. Sanctification is not some kind of elusive goal to be pursued only by "supersaints." It's an essential part of the faith walk. The Hebrew author established a tone of urgency when he wrote, "Make every effort to live in peace with all men and to be holy; without holiness no one will see the Lord" (Hebrews 12:14).

What Is Sanctification?

Our English word *sanctification* is a derivative of the Latin *sanctus facere*, which means "to make holy." Such English words as *holy*, *hallowed*, and *saint* belong to the same family. "To sanctify means commonly to make holy, that is to separate from the world and consecrate to God."[4]

In the Old Testament, things, places, and people that were set apart for God's purposes were said to be sanctified. Terms like *dedicated* and *consecrated* express the same central idea. In Exodus 29:43-44, the tent of meeting, the altar, Aaron, and his sons were all said to be sanctified. The author of 2 Kings reported that the Babylonians "took away the pots, shovels, wick trimmers, dishes and all the bronze articles used in the temple service. The commander of the imperial guard took away the censers and the sprinkling bowls—all that were made of pure gold or silver" (2 Kings 25:14-15). The national sense of humiliation over the loss of this equipment was deplored in the language of Jeremiah:

> In the days of her affliction and wandering
> Jerusalem remembers all the treasures
> that were hers in days of old (Lamentations 1:7).

The Hebrew people weren't concerned about Babylon's domination of the gold and silver market. They were humiliated because the vessels described in 2 Kings 25 were sanctified materials that had been set apart for use in God's holy temple.

In the New Testament, the emphasis shifts to people. Paul addressed his first letter to the Corinthian Christians, "To the church of God in Corinth, to those *sanctified* in Christ Jesus and called to be *holy*" (1 Corinthians 1:2, emphasis added). The Ephesian elders were addressed as sanctified men: "Now I commit you to God and to the word of his grace, which can build you up and give you an inheritance among all those who are sanctified" (Acts 20:32). In Hebrews 2:11, men were said to be holy.

The New Testament actually uses the term *sanctification* in two different senses. First, there is a sense in which conversion to Christ sanctifies us. In the context of his discussion on willful sin, the Hebrew author asked, "How much more severely do you think a man deserves to be punished who has trampled the Son of God under foot, who has treated as an unholy thing the blood of the covenant that *sanctified* him, and who has insulted the Spirit of Grace?" (Hebrews 10:29, emphasis added). The writer advanced the concept of sanctification occurring simultaneously with the sinner having his sins removed by the blood of Christ. Paul apparently thought along the same lines: "But you were washed, you were sanctified, you were justified in the name of the Lord Jesus Christ and by the Spirit of our God" (1 Corinthians 6:11). Kenneth Wuest calls this concept *positional sanctification*.[5] When a penitent believer is baptized into Christ, he touches the blood of the Savior, and in that same act, he is sanctified.

This helps us to understand why Paul addressed the Corinthian church as a sanctified body. Lifestyles within the Corinthian fellowship left much to be desired, but as recipients of God's grace, the members had become positionally sanctified. The same thing is true in the life of every sinner whose guilt has been cleansed by the blood of Christ: "There is now no condemnation for those who are in Christ Jesus" (Romans 8:1). Consequently, none of our past sins can ever be held against us since the blood of Jesus has cleansed, justified, and sanctified us. In addition, none of our present sins can ever be held against us if we continue to live under the protection of Christ's blood: "But if we walk in the light, as he is in the light, we have fellowship with one another, and the blood of Jesus, his Son, purifies us from all sin" (1 John 1:7). The same blood that sanctifies us positionally maintains us positionally in a state of sanctification. KBut this maintenance is conditional upon our willingness to "walk in the light."

Second, there is a sense in which sanctification must be viewed as *progressive*. Wuest comments,

> The work of the Holy Spirit in the yielded saint in which the believer is set apart for God in his experience by eliminating sin for his life and producing fruit, a process which goes on continually throughout the believer's life is called progressive sanctification.[6]

Paul wrote to a group of Christians in Thessalonica who had already been positionally sanctified, but he urged them to concentrate on their progressive sanctification: "May God himself, the God of peace, sanctify you through and through" (1 Thessalonians 5:23).

Positional sanctification actually becomes the platform on which progressive sanctification is erected. As Paul wrote in 2 Corinthians 3:18, we "are being transformed into [the Lord's] likeness." No Christian can claim to have reached the optimum level of sanctification. Instead of feeling superior to persons who may be struggling at a lower level, the sensitive child of God understands that he is still in the progressive stage—regardless of the number of years he has been a Christian, the level of knowledge he has acquired, or the number of good deeds he has performed.

A man and a little boy were having a discussion. The older person asked, "Son, who made you?" The little fellow replied, "To tell the truth, Mister, I ain't done yet." That pretty well describes the condition of every growing child of God. We are all somewhere on the road to maturity.

Growing Christians never view sanctification as an optional action. If baptism for the remission of sins is essential to salvation, then so is sanctification. That's not to say we'll be granted entry through the gates of heaven as a reward for our sanctification efforts. Salvation is still by grace from beginning to end. Bridges declares, "Holiness, then, is not a condition of salvation—that would be salvation by works—but a part of salvation that is received by faith in Christ."[7] Progressive sanctification is a necessary response to grace, not an avenue of qualification.

Entire Sanctification

We've already noted that the subject of sanctification ignites sparks when theological heavyweights exchange their views on it. Luther saw sanctification as an inward act of transformation, accompanied by the indwelling Spirit. Calvin was strong on self-discipline, which is odd in view of his predestination theories. Wesley believed in an instantaneous act that completely transforms an individual into the likeness of Christ.[8] The concept of entire sanctification receives its greatest emphasis in the Wesleyan tradition. Both admirers and detractors tend to misunderstand Wesley, though. Some represent him as having had little use for progressive sanctification. Actually, he believed in and encouraged the concept of gradual sanctification. On the other hand, he also believed that a person must pass through an experience of complete sanctification before being allowed entry into heaven. He envisioned a second work of grace to complete the sanctification process:

> It is thus that we wait for "entire sanctification," for full salvation from our sins. . . . As to the means, I believe this perfection is wrought in the soul by the simple act of faith; consequently in an instant. But I believe in a gradual work both preceding and following that instant. As to time, I believe the instant generally is the instant of death, the moment before the soul leaves the body. And I believe that it can be ten, twenty or forty years before.[9]

The Scriptures never speak of this dramatic, transforming instant. The New Testament picture of sanctification concentrates on progressive perfecting. The Hebrew writer exhorted his readers, "Therefore let us leave the elementary teachings about Christ and go on to maturity" (Hebrews 6:1). According to Paul, the promises of God provide the children of God with the incentive to purify "ourselves from everything that contaminates body and spirit, perfecting holiness out of reverence for God" (2 Corinthians 7:1).

Wesley was correct in recognizing that "we shall be like [God]" (1 John 3:2) when we take our place in heaven. The final act of transformation doesn't take place in this life. Paul wrote about a good work that was begun among the Philippians that would be carried "on to completion until the day of Christ Jesus" (Philippians 1:6). Until our hearts stop pulsating, our lungs cease breathing, and our brain waves go flat, we will be in the transformation process.

Fantasy or Reality

During my high-school days, I participated in a magazine subscription drive. My career as a magazine salesman started out with a burst of enthusiasm. Armed with a fistful of subscription blanks, I set off down the street to represent *Farm and Ranch* magazine. The magazine people were smart enough to know that the Future Farmers of America wouldn't go out and peddle magazines just to help out the local FFA chapter. They dangled a carrot on the end of a stick in the form of a shotgun. If memory serves me correctly, they said they would give any young man a shotgun who could sell 100 subscriptions.

I never stopped to think about the fact that there were only about 900 people in the entire town, and that 50 boys were about to descend on the small community like a horde of locusts. I didn't do too badly on the first day, but after that, I ran out of aunts, uncles, and cousins who were willing to help an enterprising young magazine sales representative. By the end of the first week, the whole community had been contacted—several times over no doubt. I soon realized the facts of life. Simple mathematics told me that my goal was next to impossible. The goal of acquiring a shotgun was little more than a fantasy.

It's important to know the difference between fantasy and reality. Christianity deals in practical reality. If people think of sanctification as an unreachable goal, they'll inevitably become discouraged and stop pursuing the process of perfecting themselves. Much of the low-grade discipleship plaguing contemporary churches can be attributed to a belief that imitating the example of Christ is far beyond the reach of the average Christian. I know people who have left the church and have taken up immoral living patterns because they thought Christian discipleship required more than they could give. I also know people who have been brought to conviction concerning their need for Jesus, but they've never turned to Him because they don't believe they can regiment themselves to a Christian lifestyle. To them, the sanctified life is a fantasy, a pipe dream. It has nothing to do with reality.

If we're to help people who get caught in these dilemmas, we must move beyond the areas of theoretical debate and deal with matters of practical application. To some people, holy living simply means giving up smoking, drinking, profanity, dancing, mixed swimming, and on and on. To be sure, there is a distinctive Christian lifestyle. Peter said of the Christian, "He does not live the rest of his earthly life for evil human desires, but rather the will of God. For you have spent enough time in the past doing what pagans choose to do—living in debauchery, lust, drunkenness, orgies, carousing and detestable idolatry" (1 Peter 4:2-3).

Unfortunately, many of the people who feel threatened by the demands of the Christian lifestyle have heard only the negatives. Also, they may have witnessed the example of professing Christians who abstained from all the aforementioned taboos but committed atrocious violations of Christian ethics in terms of disposition and attitude. Sometimes the taboos laid down in the pulpit and the classroom have the support of Scripture. At other times, they are based on questionable methods of biblical interpretation, at best, and reflect an egocentric desire to tell other people what to do, at worst. If a person has been subjected to moralizing by someone who has assumed tyrannical control over the lives of other people, it's not very likely that he is going to come away from that experience with a positive view of Christian discipleship.

Paul counterbalanced the negative restraint that's inherent in the Christian lifestyle with a positive challenge: "Do not conform any longer to the pattern of this world, but be transformed by the renewing of your mind. Then you will be able to test and approve what God's will is—his good, pleasing and perfect will" (Romans 12:2). But how do we manage this spectacular transformation? Is it really possible? Or is it tougher than selling 100 subscriptions to *Farm and Ranch* in a community of 900 people?

We start by understanding that sanctification is a goal that can never be achieved through human effort. No Christian is clever enough, bold enough, strong enough, and pure enough to make himself Christ-like. Sanctification has to be a grace response: "For the *grace of God* that brings salvation has appeared to all men. It *teaches us* to say 'No' to ungodliness and worldly passions, and to live self-controlled, upright and godly lives in this present age" (Titus 2:11-12, emphasis added). According to Ephesians 4:7-13, the grace of God provided the leadership gifts in the church set in place for the "perfecting of the saints" (KJV). Ephesians 5:26 notes that Christ does the sanctifying work.

The Holy Spirit also gets involved in the process. There will be a fuller discussion of the Holy Spirit and grace in chapter 12. But here, it's important to note that a part of the Holy Spirit's work is that of aiding the Christian in progressive sanctification: "For if you live according to the sinful nature, you will die; but if by the Spirit you put to death the misdeeds of the body, you will live" (Romans 8:13). Paul viewed the Spirit as an enabler: "I pray that out of his glorious riches he may strengthen you with power through his Spirit in your inner being" (Ephesians 3:16). The comments of John Murray are particularly insightful with respect to the Spirit's role in sanctification:

> It is the distinctive prerogative of the Holy Spirit to abide in believers, to work effectually in their whole personality, to the end that they might be filled with all the fullness of God and attain to the goal appointed for them. Sanctification progresses not by some law of psychology but by the indwelling and constantly renewing activity of the Holy Spirit.[10]

If the work of the Holy Spirit is a process that God performs for us, then how do we reconcile such passivity with the command to "purify ourselves from everything that contaminates body and spirit" (2 Corinthians 7:1)? Although God is willing to provide all the necessary instruction and even the resources needed for personal discipline, He does not bypass the human will. Sanctification, like salvation, is for "whosoever will" (Revelation 22:17, KJV).

> The Holy Spirit never does our thinking for us, nor does he express our faith. This is for individual humans. He helps us, but we always have to make up our own minds. We must furnish the faith and the commitment. He will not permit Satan to overpower us with temptation, but neither will he himself overpower us with responsible obligation to choose rightly on behalf of our own good.[11]

How Sanctification Affects Life

The sanctified life counters skeptical arguments with more eloquence than syllogisms, debate briefs, and books on apologetics. An unbeliever thought he would have some fun with one of his old drinking buddies who had recently mended his ways. The reformed drinker had forsaken the camaraderie of the tavern for the domestic life. He was now a responsible husband and father, and he could be found sitting on one of the pews in the church building on Sunday mornings. His former drinking partner chided him about his association with the church. "Do you really believe that nonsense about Jesus turning the water into wine?" the man asked. The new Christian was at a loss to know how to handle such skeptical arguments, so he simply said, "I don't know about that, my friend, but I do know he changed beer into groceries at our house." There is no effective counterargument to that kind of change in a human life.

On the other hand, no argument will successfully overcome the poor example of a person who claims to be a Christian, but who leaves the practice of Christian living behind in the church parking lot. As Sheldon Vanauken has observed,

> The best argument for Christianity is Christians; their joy, their certainty, their completeness. But the strongest argument against Christianity is also Christians—when they are sombre and joyless, when they are self righteous and smug in complacent consecration, when they are narrow and repressive, Christianity dies a thousand deaths.[12]

Summary and Conclusion

Although sanctification isn't one of the most popular subjects in Christian circles, we cannot afford to confine all discussion of the subject to the academic environment. To be sanctified is to renounce allegiance to this world and to allow one's self to be devoted to God. In the Old Testament, the word *sanctification* is commonly used with regard to things, places, and people. In the New Testament, the emphasis centers on people.

The New Testament approaches individual sanctification from two perspectives. Sometimes the New Testament writers are thinking about *positional sanctification,* which refers to the special relationship that a person develops with God when he first puts on Christ in the act of baptism. There is also a concept of *progressive sanctification,* which involves the lifelong task of spiritual discipline and growth.

The Wesleyan tradition advocates a doctrine of *entire sanctification.* The tradition points to the reception of a second work of grace at some time during the Christian's earthly pilgrimage in which one is perfected all at once. The Wesleyan tradition misses the fact that the Word of God is virtually silent concerning any such instantaneous, perfecting work of grace.

The most practical challenge confronting today's Christian is that of "perfecting holiness out of reverence for God." This becomes a discouraging demand if it is seen entirely as a work of human effort. We are essentially passive in the transformation process. Our work consists of allowing God to transform us.

The credibility of Christians, in the eyes of the non-Christian, depends on our willingness to allow God to "mold us and make us." There is no effective rebuttal to a truly sanctified life, but there is no defense for the uncommitted life.

> The soul that on Jesus
> Hath leaned for repose,
> I will not, I will not
> Desert to his foes;
> That soul, though all hell
> Shall endeavor to shake,
> I'll never, no never,
> No never forsake.
> —George Keith

Thought Questions

1. Why do people seem to have so little interest in sanctification?
2. What does *sanctification* mean? Why do people make statements like, "I'm certainly no saint"?
3. What is meant by positional sanctification?
4. What is meant by progressive sanctification?
5. What weaknesses do you see in the doctrine of entire sanctification?
6. Why does sanctification appear to be an impossible goal for many people?
7. What is the connection between sanctification and grace?
8. How does Jesus sanctify us?
9. How does the Holy Spirit sanctify us?
10. How does sanctification establish credibility for the claims of Christ in the eyes of an unbelieving world?

Notes

[1]Cary N. Weisiger, III, *The Reformed Doctrine of Sanctification* (Washington, D.C.: Christianity Today, n.d.), p. 3.

[2]*The World Book Dictionary*, 1971 ed., s.v. "Sanctification," "Sanctimonious."

[3]Jerry Bridges, *The Pursuit of Holiness* (Colorado Springs, Colo.: NavPress, 1978), p. 99.

[4]*International Standard Bible Encyclopedia*, s.v. "Sanctification" by Harris Franklin Rall.

[5]Kenneth Wuest, *Studies in the Vocabulary of the Greek New Testament* (Grand Rapids, Mich.: Eerdmans, 1945), p. 31.

[6]Ibid.

[7]Bridges, *Pursuit of Holiness*, p. 39.

[8]*Evangelical Dictionary of Theology*, s.v. "Sanctification" by R. E. O. White.

[9]John Wesley, *By John Wesley*, ed. T. Otto Nalls (New York: Association Press, 1961), pp. 91-92.

[10]John Murray, "Sanctification," *Christianity Today*, May 11, 1962.

[11]J. D. Thomas, *The Biblical Doctrine of Grace* (Abilene, Tex.: Biblical Research Press, 1977), p. 66.

[12]Sheldon Vanauken, *A Severe Mercy* (New York: Harper and Row, 1977), p. 85.

The Holy Spirit and Grace

Recently, I flew to the South Pacific for two weeks of missionary activity. At various points along the way, immigration officials asked to see my passport. When our Hawaiian Airlines flight landed at Pago Pago, American Samoa, those of us who deplaned were required to wait for about an hour and a half for workers to unload our luggage. Only then were we allowed to clear customs. While we were waiting, I struck up a conversation with a young man who had been seated just behind me on the flight from Honolulu. At first, I judged him to be a fellow American. He was Caucasian; he wore familiar, American-looking clothes. Besides that, I noticed a California address attached to his carry-on luggage. However, my judgment was mistaken. He had indeed spent six months living in California, which explained a lot of things about him, but the man turned out to be an Australian. I soon learned that it's possible to look like an American, dress like an American, and even talk like an American—and yet not be an American. Clothes don't establish citizenship, and an address label doesn't reveal nationality. One needs a passport to establish his true identity when he's traveling abroad.

The sinner who is saved by grace has a passport to establish his identity as a child of God. That passport is called the Holy Spirit. In Romans 8:16, Paul supported this basic idea: "The Spirit himself testifies with our spirit that we are God's children." In the Ephesian letter, Paul described the Holy Spirit as a seal:

> And you also were included in Christ when you heard the word of truth, the gospel of your salvation. Having believed, you were marked in him with a seal, the promised Holy Spirit, who is a deposit guaranteeing our inheritance until the redemption of those who are in God's possession—to the praise of his glory (Ephesians 1:13-14).

William Barclay observed,

> In the ancient world—and it is a custom which is still followed—when a sack or a crate or a package was despatched, it was sealed with a seal in order to guarantee that it came from the sender and that it was intact. The seal indicated where the package had come from and to whom it belonged. The Holy Spirit is the seal and sign which show that a man belongs to God.[1]

How can we know that we have received the seal confirming our identity as citizens of the kingdom? Some people may base their claim for citizenship on what they feel. Emotions sway our beliefs so powerfully that one often senses he is denying reality when he elects to believe anything that conflicts with how he feels. Nevertheless, feelings can distort reality and produce erroneous conclusions. In the Old Testament story of Joseph, the older sons of Jacob fabricated a lie to cover up their misconduct. They told their father that a wild animal had killed his favorite son. Jacob believed the contrived tale and suffered all the grief emotions that any father would suffer over the loss of a son. However, subsequent history proved that Jacob's feelings were mistaken. When one assumes that he has received God's grace on the basis of what he feels, he is using a flawed measuring device to gauge his status.

Others may say that baptism is the real measuring rod. If you are baptized by immersion and for the right reason, i.e., baptism for the remission of sins, then you can lay legitimate claim to citizenship in God's kingdom. Baptism is a definite biblical command, but is it not possible to go through the ceremony with an unbelieving heart? A person may agree to be baptized in order to please a relative. Another may see baptism as a church law requirement, which must be adhered to in order to qualify for membership. Someone else may agree to baptism as a result of being pushed into a corner by an overly aggressive soul winner. People like that don't usually undergo any kind of heart transformation. I once talked with a person who described his conversion this way, "I went into the water a dry sinner and I came out a wet sinner."

Changed Lives Prove Convincing Evidence

Genuine conversion must result in genuine change: "Therefore, if anyone is in Christ, he is a new creation; the old has gone, the new has come!" (2 Corinthians 5:17). Some years ago, I had the privilege of leading a man to Christ whose life soon began to show evidence of transformation. Shortly after his conversion, I was visiting with the new Christian's mother-in-law. In the course of the conversation, she said, "Frank doesn't seem like the same man." Of course he didn't. The grace of God had changed him.

Paul gave "before" and "after" pictures of the Christians at Ephesus. The "before" picture was drawn in Ephesians 2:1-3. He talked about following "the ways of this world" and "gratifying the cravings of [the] sinful nature." Then came Christ. Twice (vv. 5 and 8), he attributed their salvation to grace. But how did he know they were true Christians? Their life transformation provided tangible evidence: "For we are God's workmanship, created in Christ Jesus to do good works, which God prepared in advance for us to do" (Ephesians 2:10). Their changed lives demonstrated the genuineness of their conversion, but the change had not been brought about through their ingenuity and energy. They were "being built together to become a dwelling in which God lives by his Spirit" (Ephesians 2:22). The Holy Spirit energized the life-building process. Paul said they were being strengthened "through his Spirit in your inner being" (Ephesians 3:16).

Transformation is more of a process than it is a dramatic and instantaneous change. Some time ago, I drove through part of Wisconsin on Interstate 90. At one point, I passed a sign that read, HIGHWAY UNDER CONSTRUCTION. Shortly thereafter, I was forced to leave the interstate and drive twenty-five miles on a narrow two-lane detour. The Christian life is like that; it's always under construction. In Philippians 3:14, Paul spoke of pressing on toward the heavenward goal. Of course, if you see a highway construction sign and farmers are still raising corn in the right of way, you have some basis for questioning the accuracy of the claim. Similarly, when a person claims that he is saved by grace and that he is being transformed by the Holy Spirit, we can reasonably expect to see some external evidence of change. The change will be something like the surprising behavior modification that Frank's mother-in-law observed.

If there is no evidence of change, two possibilities exist. Either the person who is claiming the salvation experience was not serious about his profession of faith, or his attention was diverted from his original goal. Jesus spoke of a person who receives the Word, "But since he has no root, he lasts only a short time. When trouble or persecution comes because of the word, he quickly falls away" (Matthew 13:21).

The Holy Spirit—the Christian's Energy Source

The young lady described in the introduction to the book felt unsaved despite her commitment to a high level of discipleship. She was attempting to transform her life by using her own resources. A conscience-stricken legalist places himself between the opposing jaws of an unyielding vise; on the one hand, he believes that his God demands perfect performance, but on the other hand, he's attempting to respond to those demands through his own inadequate resources. The more he learns about the biblical requirements, the more he becomes sensitized to his own shortcomings. There is no way out of this dilemma. Landon Saunders identified a source of much frustration within the church when he wrote, "The church worries about itself. It is fretful. Protective. Fearful for tomorrow. It clings to itself."[2]

God's answer to our inadequacy is the Holy Spirit: "For if you live according to the sinful nature, you will die; but if by the Spirit you put to death the misdeeds of the body, you will live" (Romans 8:13). Perhaps we are reluctant to draw on this promised resource because the aura of mystery and the thrust of controversy are associated with the Holy Spirit. I don't claim to be able to unravel all the mystery and I certainly don't have the last word on the controversies, but I'm convinced we would be happier and we would also be more Christ-like if we better understood the Holy Spirit as a transformation resource.

Jesus said, "Whoever believes in me, as the Scripture has said, streams of living water will flow from within him." John clarified the meaning of His words: "By this he meant the Spirit, whom those who believed in him were later to receive. Up to that time the Spirit had not been given, since Jesus had not yet been glorified" (John 7:38-39). The passage teaches that Jesus anticipated the indwelling Spirit in a way that was totally different from all previous experience.

> This passage clearly shows that the believer did not possess the Holy Spirit until after the new covenant was established. Therefore, this could not have reference to the written word, for the Spirit had already operated on the minds of both the Jews and the Patriarchs through the word.[3]

Peter promised "the gift of the Holy Spirit" to those who repent and are baptized (Acts 2:38). The Holy Spirit has been given to all those who obey God (Acts 5:32), and "God has poured out his love into our hearts by the Holy Spirit, whom he has given us" (Romans 5:5). According to 1 Thessalonians 4:8, God gives us the Holy Spirit. To dispel any of our doubts, Paul pointed out, "Because you are sons, God sent the Spirit of his Son into our hearts, the Spirit who calls out, 'Abba, Father' " (Galatians 4:6).

Why did God give us the Spirit? Does He abide in us for no reason? Are we to assume that God's precious gift just lies inert within the earthly temple? Most certainly not. The Spirit "helps us in our weakness" (Romans 8:26). He also interprets our inadequate prayers and intercedes for us (Romans 8:26-27). The Spirit's power can be tapped into as an energy source (Ephesians 3:16). Through the Spirit, we are able to produce the "fruit of the Spirit" (Galatians 5:22-23).

The transformed life becomes a reality when we have formed kinship with God through His Son, Jesus Christ: "The Spirit himself testifies with our spirit that we are God's children" (Romans 8:16). The Spirit enables us to understand that we have a new kind of relationship with God. We don't even strain credibility to call it a family tie. According to Romans 8:15, it is by the Spirit that "we cry, 'Abba, Father.' " The term *abba* is an Aramaic expression, which was the first word that a Jewish child would learn to say when addressing his father.

> It is a term of endearment and intimacy. It is not the Jewish cry of Jehovah. It is not the Gentile cry of creator. It is not the distant and formal names that an outsider ascribes to deity. It is something new and intimate. It is a family name. It is a personal name.[4]

The implications of the promise are staggering. The Christian has been given the privilege of housing the Holy Spirit within his own body. The Spirit confirms a Christian's identity just as certainly as a passport establishes a citizen's identity at the customs booth. Furthermore, the Father is not an overbearing tyrant whom everyone tries to avoid. He is *Abba*, a warm, loving, and personal Father who invites us to "approach the throne of grace with confidence, so that we may receive mercy and find grace to help us in our time of need" (Hebrews 4:16).

How Can We Recognize the Spirit's Presence?

Knowledge of the Holy Spirit's presence in our lives is a matter of faith. The Holy Spirit can't be weighed, calibrated, or gauged by human measuring devices. We know the Spirit dwells within us because we trust the promises of the God who revealed His will to us on the pages of the New Testament.

The Scriptures nowhere teach that the presence of the Spirit is to be confirmed by human feelings. To be sure, God created our emotions. A surge of emotional joy must certainly come to the heart of any person who realizes that Jesus has "cleansed our soul from sin; sent the Spirit within." However, feelings can be misleading.

Miraculous signs do not indicate the presence of the Holy Spirit. Some Christians in the early church were endowed with the ability to perform signs and wonders. There were many Christians, however, who did not possess those gifts. "Are all apostles? Are all prophets? Are all teachers? Do all work miracles? Do all have gifts of healing? Do all speak in tongues? Do all interpret?" (1 Corinthians 12:29-30). These questions are rhetorical in nature, and the implied answer to each one is "no." It's significant to observe that John the Baptist was "filled with the Holy Spirit even from birth" (Luke 1:15). Yet the apostle John noted that "John never performed a miraculous sign" (John 10:41).

Is the mere promise of God insufficient to confirm the presence of the Holy Spirit in our lives? Let me draw a parallel between the promise of God and the promise of a secular employer. My wife works for a large hospital in the city where we live. Every other Friday, she gets paid. The hospital does not pay her in cash or by check. The money is deposited in our joint account by a computer. She receives a printout to confirm the actual amount placed on deposit. We've never gone to the bank and asked to see the actual money in the vault. We write checks on our account, and they clear the bank. We operate that way because we trust my wife's employer and also because we trust the bank.

The child of God knows the Holy Spirit abides within because the Word of God assures him that God has given the Holy Spirit as a deposit in his heavenly account. As Paul indicated, "Having believed, you were marked in him with a seal, the promised Holy Spirit, who is a deposit guaranteeing our inheritance until the redemption of those who are God's possession—to the praise of his glory" (Ephesians 1:13-14).

Although the Spirit has been placed on deposit within us, we still choose whether we will draw on our resource. In Galatians 5:22-23, Paul spoke of the "fruit of the Spirit," and we begin to appreciate the presence of the Spirit as we "write checks" against our account and develop the qualities of "love, joy, peace, patience, kindness, goodness, faithfulness, gentleness and self-control." We are warned, however, that the Spirit can be grieved (Ephesians 4:30), quenched (1 Thessalonians 5:19), insulted (Hebrews 10:29), and blasphemed (Matthew 12:31).

Perhaps the most convincing proof of the Spirit's presence in our lives is the evidence of the transformed life. Garth Black brings the matter into perspective:

> The chief work that the Holy Spirit has with Christians is to develop them into the likeness of Christ, to reproduce in them the beauty and glory of the personality of Christ. But one cannot develop the likeness of Christ without bearing the fruit of the Holy Spirit. The test of the Christian life is whether it bears the fruit of the Spirit.[5]

Summary and Conclusion

The presence of the indwelling Spirit assures the Christian of his status as a family member in God's household. Two New Testament figures of speech are used to present the concept to Bible readers. The Holy Spirit is spoken of first as a seal, certifying the authenticity of conversion, and second as a deposit, guaranteeing the blessings of God.

A changed life provides the world with the most tangible form of proof that the Christian life is genuine. The Holy Spirit is the resource that makes the transformation possible. However, the transformation is not an instantaneous acquisition; it's a lifelong process. The evidence of the transformation process is observed as the various forms of the Holy Spirit's fruit are gradually integrated into the human personality.

> Breathe, O breathe thy loving Spirit
> Into every troubled breast;
> Let us all in thee inherit;
> Let us find thy perfect rest;

Take away the love of sinning,
Take our load of guilt away;
End the work of thy beginning,
Bring us to eternal day.
—Charles Wesley

Thought Questions

1. What message is conveyed when the Scriptures speak of the Holy Spirit as a seal? As a deposit?
2. To what extent should Christians rely on their feelings?
3. How does the Holy Spirit testify that we are God's children?
4. How much change must take place before conversion? What about afterward?
5. How does the Holy Spirit provide power for daily Christian living?
6. Why do Christians receive the gift of the Holy Spirit at baptism?
7. Why does the conscience-stricken legalist often become discouraged in his efforts to live the Christian life?
8. What does the expression "Abba, Father" mean to us in practical terms?
9. How can we know the Spirit lives in us?
10. Consider the pros and cons of the two prevailing theories concerning the indwelling of the Holy Spirit, i.e., indwelling through the written word alone and the actual personal indwelling.

Notes

[1]William Barclay, *The Daily Study Bible—The Letters to the Galatians and Ephesians*, 2d ed. (Edinburgh: Saint Andrew Press, 1958), pp. 100-101.

[2]Landon Saunders, "Church Renewal—How?" *The Church and the Future* (Abilene, Tex.: Abilene Christian College Bookstore, 1972), p. 91.

[3]Garth W. Black, *The Holy Spirit* (Abilene, Tex.: Biblical Research Press, 1967), p. 83.

[4]Richard Rogers, "The Free Man in Christ," *Freedom in Christ* (Abilene, Tex.: Abilene Christian College Bookstore, 1976), pp. 112-13.

[5]Black, *Holy Spirit*, p. 55.

Blessed Assurance

At the beginning of the book, I mentioned a woman who came to my office to discuss her feelings about salvation. At the time she talked with me, she felt very little assurance. She was trying to maintain high moral standards. She was in the assembly every time the church doors opened. She even had an intellectual understanding concerning salvation by grace, but she had never been able to internalize it. There are many like her, including some of God's most precious saints who are spending their last years in physical decline. At a time when they should be anticipating going home to be with God, they are often fearful of the future. All their lives, they've heard preaching about what they must do in order to become eligible for entrance into heaven.

Not long ago, I attended the funeral of my uncle. He was a fine man, and I looked up to him as something of a role model in my younger years. He was a great student of the Bible, a kind, compassionate, and generous man. He had served as an elder in the church at one time. After his death, several members of his family and some friends were sitting around the kitchen table recalling memories as people often do in their grief. Several comments were made concerning his life and his example. After awhile, someone made a statement that I have heard repeated many times among Christians. It went something like this: "He was such a good man. If he didn't make it to heaven, nobody will."

Every person there was either a friend or a relative, so I decided not to let that statement go unchallenged. I said, "I believe my uncle is going to heaven, but he's not going to heaven because he was a good man. He was certainly one of the best men I ever knew, but that goodness is not enough to get him into heaven. My uncle is going to heaven because he was a child of God, and because Jesus Christ died on the cross for his sins."

My friends and relatives found it necessary to attach my uncle's track record to their feelings of hope because they had been exposed to teaching that connected salvation with what a person does. Preachers in the Restoration Movement have typically emphasized the importance of obedience in their sermons. They have reacted to the view of justification by faith, which separates faith from action. A negative response to an inactive faith is appropriate. One must remember, however, that the doctrine of justification by faith alone is itself a reaction to the doctrine of salvation by meritorious works. We should not offer a modified program of salvation by works as an alternative to the doctrine of justification by faith alone. Such an emphasis ignores the grace-faith principle on the one hand, but it also makes Christianity a source of misery and fear on the other hand. God never has intended for Christians to go through life questioning their salvation. The Word of God speaks clearly on this matter: "I write these things to you who believe in the name of the Son of God so that you may know that you have eternal life" (1 John 5:13).

Why It's Important to Feel Saved

The Word of God doesn't require us to feel saved in order to be saved. On the contrary, the Scriptures teach that we can actually be saved even when our feelings are in the opposite direction: "This then is how we know that we belong to the truth, and how we set our hearts at rest in his presence whenever our hearts condemn us. For God is greater than our hearts, and he knows everything" (1 John 3:19-20).

Yet it is important to feel saved. John continued the same thought by pointing out, "Dear friends, if our hearts do not condemn us, we have confidence before God." It's pretty difficult for a Christian to maintain good mental health when he starts out every day with doubts and fears about his eternal destiny.

It's impossible to experience good mental health without some degree of confidence. It's generally agreed by experts in the field of mental health that inward peace can be achieved only when a person's behavior conforms to his value system. Frank B. Minirth and Paul D. Meier serve as president and vice-president of the Minirth-Meier Psychiatric Clinic in Richardson, Texas. They have observed, "Doing what is wrong lowers our self-worth. Doing what is right greatly improves our self-worth. In our experience as psychiatrists, when people have told us they feel guilty, it is usually true guilt. They feel guilty because they are guilty."[1]

Of course if we lived in perfect conformity to our values 100 percent of the time, we would have every reason to feel confident about our relationship with God. Our problem stems from the fact that none of us can do this. John noted, "If we claim to be without sin, we deceive ourselves and the truth is not in us" (1 John

1:8). That's why we need a Savior. The basis of our confidence has nothing to do with our perfect performance. If we never committed a sin, then eternal life would be ours to claim as a result of our perfect obedience, but near misses don't count. Someone has said, "Close only counts in horseshoes and atom bomb attacks." The basis of our security, then, has to rest on the work of Christ.

Strangely enough, however, our capacity for obedience increases when we learn to internalize grace and start believing that we are saved people. In 1 John 3:21-22, we are told, "Dear friends, if our hearts do not condemn us, we have confidence before God and receive from him anything we ask, because we obey his commands and do what pleases him." John has described a supportive cycle. Obedience establishes confidence, and confidence enhances obedience.

Our evangelistic effectiveness goes up when we feel confident about our salvation. When we're just "hoping" that we might be saved, we communicate our uncertainty to others. It's very difficult to say to a person who is not a Christian, "Why don't you become a Christian so you can be just as filled with doubts and fears about your future as I am?" On the other hand, when we develop real confidence about our relationship with God, other people begin to wonder about how they can be like us in that regard.

Robert Shank tells of a conversation between a banker and his client, a successful businessman. The banker began the conversation by asking, "What do you know for sure?" Without hesitation, his client responded, "I know the blood of Jesus Christ cleanses me from all sin, I'm a child of God by faith, and I'm on my way to heaven." That wasn't exactly what the banker expected this businessman to say, but he was impressed. He said, "Come into my office. I want to talk with you." During the next few minutes, the businessman had the privilege of talking about Jesus with this influential man from the financial world.[2]

Why Is There So Much Insecurity in the Church?

Our lack of assurance has probably developed from many different roots. Every individual is unique, and any person who attempts to know all the reasons is probably just a bit arrogant. I'm sure some of the insecurity that exists among Christians today is deeply imbedded in personality problems that remain unknown outside the person who harbors those feelings. Nevertheless, we can speak in generalities and pinpoint some of the problems.

1. *Insecurity exists when people go too far in trying to respond to the "once saved always saved" theory.* The doctrine of "the perseverance of the saints" originated in the theology of John Calvin. Calvin believed that people are saved as the result of a unilateral action of God in which God arbitrarily selects certain persons to be saved and certain persons to be lost prior to their existence on the earth. Therefore, he realized that, logically, he would have to conclude that a saved person never walks away from the grace of God.

Scholars and teachers within the Restoration Movement have uniformly rejected the conclusions of Calvin—and properly so. The Scriptures make it clear that the entire process of election is conditional. Paul wrote, "But now he has reconciled you by Christ's physical body through death to present you holy in his sight, without blemish and free from accusation—if you continue in your faith, established and firm, not moved from the hope held out in the gospel" (Colossians 1:22-23). In words as plain as language can make it, Paul said that our salvation is conditional, and the condition is that of our continuing in the faith. However, we must not reject the Calvinistic view of eternal security in exchange for a doctrine of no security. One conclusion is almost as bad as the other. It's been said that even though the Bible doesn't teach the doctrine of "once saved always saved," neither does it teach the doctrine of "once saved barely saved."

2. *Some of our insecurity probably stems from a misunderstanding of the way forgiveness takes place.* Many people in restoration churches hold to the doctrine of the "second law of pardon," which goes something like this. When a Christian sins, he falls from grace and remains lost until he repents and asks God to forgive him. The Christian who sins every day is lost for part of that day. God is constantly erasing and reinstating our names in the Lamb's book of life. We must know and obey all the truth in God's Word to be saved. The only way to be saved is to "die in your streak." It's too bad if a careless driver cuts you off at an intersection and you momentarily allow an evil thought to enter your mind just before the ensuing crash sends you into eternity. It's pretty difficult to live a confident life with that set of theological beliefs.

3. *A false sense of humility causes some to doubt their salvation.* Certain biblical teachings come to mind as one thinks about the subject of humility: "Pride goes before destruction, a haughty spirit before a fall" (Proverbs 16:18), and "So if you think you are standing firm, be careful that you don't fall" (1 Corinthians 10:12). Many

of us have been turned off by the breast-beating tactics of those who flaunt their assurance. We find such an attitude less than admirable and contrary to the spirit of Christ. Consequently, we overcompensate and try to distance ourselves from such arrogance.

4. *Guilt-oriented teaching takes its toll.* We have often encountered a pulpit style in which guilt is used as the primary tool for motivation. Several years ago, a good sister in the church told me, "I don't come to church to hear how good I am. I come to church to hear about what's wrong with me." Some of us develop a sort of masochistic mentality. We seem to think there's virtue in being willing to subject ourselves to verbal bombardment from the pulpit week after week. It's not easy to feel confident about much of anything when your entire diet of spiritual food is provided by someone in an attack posture.

How Can We Know for Sure?

There's absolutely no question about the fact that God wants us to feel a sense of security. The Hebrew writer said, "Let us draw near to God with a sincere heart in full assurance of faith, having our hearts sprinkled to cleanse us from a guilty conscience and having our bodies washed with pure water" (Hebrews 10:22). The problem for insecure Christians is knowing how to leap the chasm between the promise of assurance and the awareness of personal sinfulness. Before suggesting a basis for developing our sense of security, we need to look at some faulty approaches.

1. *Security is not based on how we feel.* Feelings are extremely unreliable and inconsistent. That's why John

reminds us that God is greater than our hearts. Robert Shank observes, "When we begin to determine our spiritual status and to define our doctrines by human experience, feelings and opinions, we have embarked on a path of error, the end of which is everlasting disaster."[3]

2. *Heritage is an inadequate approach to security.* That was the problem of the first-century Jew. He thought he was righteous because Abraham's blood flowed through his veins, but Paul contradicted that when he wrote, "Jews and Gentiles alike are all under sin" (Romans 3:9). Some of us play our own heritage game. We rely either on our family heritage or on our Restoration Movement as the basis of our confidence.

3. *Past conversion is not an adequate basis for present security.* If you were to ask some Christians to give a reason for the hope that they have, many would point to their baptism. Indeed, baptism does mark the time when one puts off the old self and puts on the new self, but what is your current status as a child of God? And if your status is one of assurance, what is it based on? Baptism is important, but it doesn't provide the Christian with sustained assurance throughout his entire life.

A Proper Understanding

We must start with the understanding that our position of favor in God's sight is determined by what Christ has done and not by anything that we have done. Romans 5:6 speaks directly to our condition: "You see, at just the right time, when we were still powerless, Christ died for the ungodly." Salvation is not based on the principle of the survival of the fittest. Salvation is offered to those who aren't and who can never be the fittest. That's precisely what grace is all about; grace is unmerited favor.

The gospel says that God longs for a relationship with us, even though we aren't worthy to enter into that relationship. I've often come to the end of a Bible study only to find that the person with whom I have shared the gospel makes some statement like, "I just don't think I'm worthy to be a Christian." That person is exactly correct. It's because we aren't worthy that God sent Jesus to die on the cross. Our confidence is based on the worthiness of Jesus, not our own worthiness.

Through the Cross, God is saying to us "I love you unconditionally." He loves us enough to forgive us, even when we disappoint Him. He loves us enough to stay with us through the rough times. He loves us enough to keep us clean through the blood of Christ: "But if we walk in the light, as he is in the light, we have fellowship with one another, and the blood of Jesus, his Son, purifies us from all sin" (1 John 1:7).

What does it mean to "walk in the light"? J. W. Roberts offers the following insight:

> This would seem to imply that the Christian is one who is above sin as regards his conduct—one who does not sin. This John does not mean. He will go on to make the fact plain. What John explains is that walking in the light means that the blood of Jesus Christ his son cleanses us from all sin. To this end John will go on to present Jesus as an advocate and expiation (2:1, 2). This cleansing is not automatic; it implies confession (including of course, penitence and renewal, verse 9) and keeping his commandments (2:3). . . . Walking in the light implies our sincere effort not to sin. Christ's blood, under this condition, cleanses us from all sins (there

is no exception; his blood cleanses totally), and in
this way guiltless children have spiritual association
with their Father.[4]

Confession of sins does not imply that we must make
a verbal admission of sin to God following each infraction
of divine law. It has more to do with an attitude toward
sin. It suggests that we agree with God about our sins.
In other words, we remain in a confessing frame of mind.
We don't try to defend our sins. We don't rationalize
them. We don't deny them. We become confessing,
honest, open, and unpretentious people.

If we maintain that kind of mind-set and if we continue
in a lifestyle that makes a sincere effort to obey God, *we
remain continually cleansed from our sins.* We do not
temporarily fall out of grace every time we do something
wrong!

> The verb suggests that God does more than forgive;
> He erases the stain of sin. And the present tense
> shows that it is a continuous process. . . . What
> is clear is that if we walk in the light, God has
> made provision to cleanse us from whatever sin
> from what otherwise mar our fellowship with him
> or each other.[5]

First John 1:7 opens up a profound understanding to
the child of God. Sincere, God-fearing, God-serving
Christians are not lost because of their imperfection. It
is quite probable that many within the body of Christ
have never been out of grace in their entire Christian
experience. Unfortunately, a works-oriented approach to
the subject of salvation has led many of us to question
and, in some cases, deny our assurance of salvation.
People who use guilt and fear to keep others in line

must shoulder the responsibility for creating a fellowship of insecure believers. It's not wholesome. It's not encouraging. It's not Christian.

Summary and Conclusion

Does the promise of security based on the merit of Christ's saving work on the cross sound too good to be true? It's very difficult for many of us to accept the fact that God would give us anything that we don't deserve. We live in a culture in which we have been told there is no free lunch. We've come to believe that we get what we pay for. Consequently, the thought of receiving God's blessings without earning His favor runs contrary to our experiences.

Bruce Larson tells a story about vacationing with his family in Canada. He had gone fishing every morning with his two sons. Then one morning, his daughter and a friend who had accompanied her on the trip asked to go out in the boat. They caught very few fish, and after awhile, it was time to go back to the camp. Just as they were about to pull their lines in, Larson told the girls, "I'm sorry we didn't catch any big fish." At that very moment, a fifteen-inch Northern jumped out of the water, hit Larson in the face, and fell into the boat. When they got back to the camp, they told the boys what happened, but the boys wouldn't believe them. The story sounded too good to be true. Larson goes on to say, "I've told this story to a great many people and the skeptics invariably outnumber the believers."[6]

That's the problem in trying to understand the gospel story. The kind of relationship that God has offered just sounds too good to be true. Nevertheless, it is true that

God wants to accept us. He wants to call us His children. He wants to keep us in His family, even when we've messed things up. He always respects the independence of human will. We can walk away from His fellowship if that's what we want to do. He will allow us that freedom, even though it breaks His heart. Do you believe that His promises are real? "For God so loved the world that he gave his one and only Son, that whoever believes in him shall not perish but have eternal life" (John 3:16).

> Blessed assurance, Jesus is mine!
> O, what a foretaste of glory divine!
> Heir of salvation, purchase of God;
> Born of His Spirit, washed in his blood.
> —Fanny J. Crosby

Thought Questions

1. Why do Christians often insist on connecting spiritual rewards with human performance?
2. How is it possible to actually be in a saved condition without feeling assurance of salvation?
3. Why is it important to feel a sense of assurance?
4. How does a proper understanding of grace increase the probability of obedience in the life of the Christian?
5. What is your opinion of the belief that grace takes away the necessity of human responsibility?
6. How does grace affect evangelism?
7. Why are so many Christians insecure about their salvation?
8. From a grace perspective, how would you respond to the doctrine of "once saved always saved"?

9. Does the Bible justify the doctrine of "the second law of pardon"? Why or why not?
10. How can we help insecure Christians develop a greater sense of assurance?

Notes

[1]Frank B. Minirth and Paul D. Meier, *Happiness Is a Choice* (Grand Rapids, Mich.: Baker Book House, 1978), p. 70.

[2]Robert Shank, *Life in the Son* (Springfield, Mo.: Westcott Publishers, 1960), p. 287.

[3]Ibid., p. 289.

[4]J. W. Roberts, *The Living Word Commentary—The Letters of John* (Austin, Tex.: R. B. Sweet Co., 1968), p. 32.

[5]John R. W. Stott, *Tyndale New Testament Commentaries—The Epistles of John* (Leicester, England: Intervarsity Press; 1960, Grand Rapids, Mich.: Eerdmans, 1983), pp. 75-76.

[6]Bruce Larson, *No Longer Strangers* (Waco, Tex.: Word, 1971), pp. 65-66.